Women in American Protestant Religion 1800–1930

A thirty-six volume reprint collection demonstrating the breadth and diversity of the roles played by women in American religion.

EDITED BY

Carolyn De Swarte Gifford
Coordinator of the Women's History Project
General Commission on Archives and History
United Methodist Church

CONSULTING EDITOR

Donald W. Dayton
Northern Baptist Theological Seminary

A Garland Series

*Memoir
of the Late
Martha Hazeltine Smith*

Sarah Sleeper

Garland Publishing, Inc.
New York & London   1987

This facsimile has been made from a copy in the
Yale University Library.

For a complete list of the titles in this series,
see the final pages of this volume.

Library of Congress Cataloging-in-Publication Data

Sleeper, Sarah.
  Memoir of the late Martha Hazeltine Smith.

  (Women in Protestant religion, 1800-1930)
  Reprint. Originally published: Boston :
J. Smith, 1843.
  1. Smith, Martha Hazeltine, 1808-1841. 2. New
Hampton Female Seminary--History. 3. Teachers--New
Hampshire--Biography. 4. Women teachers--New
Hampshire--Biography. 5. Baptists--New Hampshire--
Biography. I. Title. II. Series.
LD7251.N25346S657 1987   373.12'0092'4 [B] 87-36612
ISBN 0-8240-0686-0

The volumes in this series are printed on
acid-free, 250-year-life paper.

Printed in the United States of America

Thayer & Co's Lith Boston.

Your affectionate friend
M. Hazeltine Smith

MEMOIR

OF THE LATE

MARTHA HAZELTINE SMITH.

BY SARAH SLEEPER,

PRINCIPAL OF THE NEW HAMPTON FEMALE SEMINARY.

> " Hath not thy voice been here among us heard !
> And that deep soul of gentleness and power,
> Have we not felt its breath in every word,
> Wont from thy lips, as Hermon's dew, to shower?
> — Yes ! in our hearts thy fervent words have burned —
> Of Heaven they were, and thither have returned."
>
> MRS. HEMANS.

———◆———

PUBLISHED BY JOSEPH SMITH.

———————

BOSTON:
PRINTED BY FREEMAN AND BOLLES.
MDCCCXLIII.

CONTENTS.

· Page.

CHAPTER V.

CHAPTER VI.

CHAPTER VII.

CHAPTER VIII.

CHAPTER IX.

CHAPTER X.

CHAPTER XI.

CHAPTER XII.

Page.

CHAPTER XXII.

CHAPTER XXIII.

MEMOIR

OF

MRS. M. HAZELTINE SMITH.

———— ———

INTRODUCTION.

We learn by example. Occasionally an original genius strikes a new path, and by unprecedented means attains at once an illustrious position. But in a majority of instances, excellence is attained by free, but persevering imitation. The educated, the influential, the honored owe not a little of their pre-eminence to the nerving influence of distinguished models.

We overlook this truth, and as we watch in the distance the acts of one who seemingly effects every purpose by an effort of the will, we class him with the illustrious few, who, by the decree of Heaven, must remain unequalled. Were the curtain withdrawn, were the net-work removed, and we admitted behind the scene, our wonder would cease, and our confidence in personal success would be aroused and

1

confirmed. A knowledge of the thought, the study, and the application which success requires, could hardly fail to produce a consciousness that personal distinction is attainable by adequate effort.

Let us not be misunderstood. To improve, is not to create. An intellect susceptible of cultivation, an active temperament, and the elements of a vigorous physical constitution are nature's gifts. With these prerequisites, the way to a sphere of extensive usefulness is accessible. Too great love of ease, too little love for distinction, and a want of the spirit of benevolence are the chief obstacles. We cannot continue to say a little more sleep, and yet be distinguished. We must be willing to sacrifice personal enjoyments, to live in an atmosphere of excitement, to be ever on the alert. Labor, responsibility and unremitted vigilance must be as things of nought, we must press on, hope on, even against hope. Our feelings must be enlisted. Deep interest fixes the attention ; attention suggests plans, and these are in the train of success. An end definitely in view, and the feelings interested, the issue is as we will. If a spirit of benevolence be united to unremitted exertion and deep interest, the result becomes highly commendable. Poverty may exert its deadening influence, envy and malice may oppose ; yet, before application, an absorbing interest, and good feeling, obstacles will vanish like dew before the sunbeams.

Of the truth of these sentiments we have a demonstration in the public career of the subject of this memoir. Unaided by the power of wealth, or public beneficence, she attained preëminent elevation among the useful of her sex. Her public life is, throughout, worthy of imitation. If those desiring similar success will learn by example to grasp her characteristic excellences, if they will mark the means by which she became both useful and honored, and pursue a like course, they may become equally distinguished.

There is another view which should interest every one, though difficult to be delineated and rendered practically beneficial. I refer to the social character. Few ladies occupy stations requiring great depth of research, power of thought, energy of purpose, and decision of character; but every one is subject to the pleasures and pains incident to social life — every one has thrilling emotions arising from social ties. Friends, confidants, counsellors, kindred! At the mere mention of these cherished words, what living thoughts rush to the mind! what deep feelings are at once awakened! But the emotions, though always exquisite, are by no means uniformly pleasant. They are not unfrequently those of exquisite anguish.

We can hardly meet an individual who has not felt grief connected with some social relation. A friend has been discarded, a confidant mistrusted, a relative blamed. But resentment, or the breaking of friendship has not cured the evil. A family, though sundered by discord, is a family still, and by the decree of Heaven must remain so. Old friends may be discarded, but they continue to sustain to us peculiar relations. They are, in some sense, a part of ourselves. Let one after another be severed, and we become as a blasted tree.

Though God has created us in His own image,

and by the gift of intellect made all created things subservient to our will, he has given us a constitution which renders it impossible to be happy without the concurrence of those around us. From these dependences must arise mutual obligations. If God has given a constitution which requires friends, he has established principles which must govern intercourse with them, one of which is, if observation may decide, *Be slow to blame the accused, prompt to distrust the accuser.* There is no perfection in fallen man. Our *dearest*, our *best*, will sometimes yield to passion and caprice, I had almost said to base, unworthy acts. Those nearest perfection will not always seem all we could desire; but blame will increase the evil. We must "hope all things, endure all things." This, our own best good and the good of those around us imperiously demand.

The social relations, in a great degree, determine the permanency of health. Labor, when accompanied by a happy frame of mind, seldom so impairs the constitution that it cannot be restored. But when the social relations are unhappy, the spirits ebb; buoyancy departs; the constitution becomes debilitated; and the victim sinks into a premature grave.

Perfection of domestic character implies the possession of every human excellence. The duties of domestic life, ever complex, ever varying, require the careful exercise of the understanding, a prudent use of knowledge, the unerring wisdom of experience, unyielding integrity of conscience, and the self-denying benevolence and overflowing charity of the heart. Around the domestic fireside, the Author of our being has made such influences to cluster as are well adapted, not only to make manifest the excellence of principles already adopted, and the propriety of habits already formed, but to nurture and ripen every germ of personal and social virtue. In no other situation are the attendant circumstances so favorable to the formation of a well-balanced character as in the domestic circle. Every branch of professional life is surrounded with certain influences peculiar to itself, which usually leave their mark, a mark consisting of peculiarities or eccentricities of character. But the mould of character presented in the varied influences of domestic life is beautifully symmetrical. No situation can be more favorable to real improvement. So God ordains. Surrounding circumstances necessarily exert upon us an irresistible influence. Though short indeed the domestic career of her whom we contemplate, happy were the results. It afforded a more favorable opportunity than she had ever before enjoyed for the promotion of personal piety. Of the piety of persons in public life, religious activity is usually the most prominent characteristic. Their attention is often so entirely absorbed in the interests of others, that there is a liability to neglect themselves. The guide of others must have good words upon the tongue, if they are not felt in the heart. Let the attention, however, be called from a too exclusive devotion to public duties, let there be time to commune with the heart, and personal piety becomes equally prominent. We should learn harmoniously to unite religious activity and personal piety.

1*

CHAPTER I.

RANK OF THE FEMALE TEACHER — MISS HAZELTINE'S
POSITION AT NEW HAMPTON — AIM IN DELINEATING
HER CHARACTER.

" A WOMAN of cultivated understanding and correct religious principle, when engaged in the responsible task of educating the rising generation, in reality fills one of the most responsible stations to which a human being can aspire." Among the aristocratic of our country it has heretofore been considered more honorable to do nothing. But this sentiment is fast passing away ; and we trust that even now, few in New England would regard lightly anything which would afford assistance in moulding the intellect, the heart, or the habits.

This consideration has induced me to attempt a delineation of the character of Mrs. M. Hazeltine Smith. Perhaps no woman in our country has been more successful in developing mind, or has exerted a more extensive or healthful influence as a teacher of young ladies. All her early sentiments, feelings, and actions tended to this one point. When she studied, it was to fit herself to impart instruction. When she wrote, it was to elevate the office of teacher, to develope the object of education, and the means for its accomplishment; and when she taught, it was in perfect unison with her precepts. In her own language she labored " to develope well the mental faculties, so as to enable them to take a large and accurate survey of the wide field of observation ; to direct the attention successively to the several departments within this range, and to assist in gathering from each a store of general principles, to be garnered in the mind for general use ; to direct in applying these principles to the conduct of human life, and in forming those habits which are to grow and strengthen with increasing years, and mould the character and destiny." In the Baptist community, while connected with the New Hampton Female Seminary, she gave a new impulse to female education.

Seventeen years ago the Baptist denomination had no literary institution in Connecticut, Massachusetts, New Hampshire or Vermont — none in New England, but Brown University and Waterville College. New Hampton Institution is the oldest Baptist Academy in the country. This school was originally designed for the benefit of the town where it is located. And at an early period was little patronized beyond its immediate vicinity. In 1825, John K. Simpson, Esq., a native of New Hampton, then a wealthy merchant in Boston, advised the trustees to place the school under the patronage of the New Hampshire Baptists. With a view to this, the churches, through his influence, were requested to elect delegates to form a convention. But only five churches in the state felt sufficient interest in education to comply with the request. Ministers, however, met on their own responsibility. A convention was formed, the proposition of the trustees accepted, and Rev. B. F. Farnsworth, then editor of the Christian Watchman, appointed principal.

Mr. Farnsworth was generally known and appreciated. Mr. Simpson's mercantile business gained him a very general acquaintance. Through the influence of these two popular and responsible men the institution attained a very extensive patronage from Massachusetts. The people of New Hampshire gradually became interested, and soon the school was thronged with pupils. Increase of numbers required an increase of accommodations, and Mr. Simpson generously stepped forward and contributed of his abundance for a new Academy building. Other friends supplied the deficit and a chapel was erected. Soon after, efficiency and strength were added to the board by the election of Josiah Quincy, Esq., as one of the trustees. With the joint contributions of Messrs. Simpson and Quincy, and generous donations from the Baptist ministers and churches in New Hampshire, and friends from abroad, a commodious boarding edifice was added to the accommodations.

In the meantime the people in the village, a mile and a half from the institution, erected a building in their own vicinity and gave it to the trustees of the institution to be occupied by the female department. A school was opened in this building in May, 1829, under the care of Miss Martha Hazeltine, principal, and Miss Rebecca Hadley, associate teacher. At this place Miss Hazeltine earned her meed of fame. This was the scene of the most interesting and important events in her career of usefulness and in her life.

Much has been said of the location of the New Hampton Female Seminary. From the general descriptions we should be prepared to see anything but the beautiful. But we should not envy the taste that could take a view at the entrance of the village just at evening and find nothing to admire. From this view, the white seminary building, and the church, with its spire glittering in the rays of the setting sun, stand at the right, far removed from the bustle of the village, in the centre of the slope of a hill presenting one surface of green sward. On the left is a chain of hills diversified with cultivated fields, rich foliage, and rural cottages. In front of the seminary building, at the base of the hill on which it is located, is a small sheet of water encircled with foliage, the head of a stream flowing along at the base of the hills on the left. The village lies in the valley in the direction from which the view is taken. The background is a sunset with a sky truly Italian.

But the chief attraction of the village is its school, and the chief attraction of the school at an early period was its distinguished principal. Miss Hazeltine impressed one at a glance, as possessing great energy and decision. She expressed this in her firm yet spirited carriage. She was rather tall, of a full round figure, fair complexion and light hair ; the latter disposed so as to exhibit to advantage a forehead naturally full and intellectual. Her pupils thought, on first acquaintance, that they should fear the stately, dignified woman too much to love. But they were mistaken. Her untiring interest, her assiduity as a teacher, her love for the souls of her pupils, uniformly gained their affections.

A history of her life, to be practically beneficial, should present the *origin* of her *usefulness, industry* and *energy;* the *manner* in which she acquired her *fund* of *knowledge;* and the *source* of her *success* in *moulding character.*

CHAPTER II.

MARTHA HAZELTINE was born at Rumney, N. H., May 19, 1808. Her father, Deacon John Hazeltine, was ever distinguished for his love of gospel truth. He read the Bible to his assembled family, as constantly as the return of morning and evening. With the simplicity which ever characterizes an evangelical Christian, he impressed its doctrines, urged its requisitions, and prayed for the Spirit's energy to prepare the heart for the reception of its gracious truths. Martha, therefore, while a child, learned to appreciate the principles of our holy religion, to apprehend the destiny of her being, and the object of her present state of existence. A reverence for Christianity, and a sense of personal duty to promote its interests, were interwoven with all her early impressions.

Her eldest sister formed for her habits of industry. This sister, in 1815, married Mr. Moses Hadley, and removed to Boston. Martha, when only seven years of age, became a member of her family. She was her sister's only reliance in household cares and was therefore diligently employed. She was accustomed to say the example and precepts of her sister had a great effect upon her in forming the habit of being always busy about something that might turn to good account. She thus learned to bring energy and perseverance to every useful labor.

While with her sister she attended one of the public schools in Boston; and there distinguished herself as a scholar, though she studied little at home, except when she could place her book before her, and still diligently employ her hands in domestic duties. "At Boston," she once remarked, "I began to thirst for literary distinction. My success at school fanned the flame of ambition. I stood at the head of my class, and that too with those above my age. Here commenced my desire for preëminence."

Her heart was yet unchanged. She had not the impulse of love to God, to urge her onward. Still she was thoughtful, and even seemed a Christian in her external character. She says, in a letter to a friend; "While I resided in Boston my conscience was tender and used to bring home truth, which I heard almost constantly at the catechetical exercises, conducted by the beloved Dr. Sharp at the Sabbath School in his society, and from the sacred desk. My judgment was fully convinced of the necessity of a change of heart, and it seemed my will was persuaded to do anything, or make any sacrifice for an assurance that I was the adopted child of God. I became very punctilious in the performance of religious duties, striving to exercise self-denial, and resignation, and to detect and mortify pride, and finally came to believe that I must have been regenerated, and cherished a hope. For two or three years I wrote my exercises daily, which, as near as I can remember, bore considerable resemblance to the matter generally contained in religious journals.

"At the age of twelve ill health induced me to return home, and two years after, while a member of my father's family, I trust my heart was really given to God. I gave up my previous hope in consequence of reading a tract entitled, 'Am I a Christian?' The question seemed to me a momentous one. After reading the tract, my full conviction was, that I was not a Christian. My anxiety returned. I felt that my condition was dangerous in the extreme, and that to continue in that situation was madness. I accordingly set about the work of conversion as I would anything else. I inquired most solemnly what I should do to be saved, and endeavored to receive the Gospel answer, but it seemed inappropriate. I thought I did believe. I then recollected that repentance was essential. Thus I endeavoured to exercise myself, by reflecting upon the goodness of God, and my abuse of that goodness, by reflecting upon particular sins, but could excite no repentance. Even the sufferings of the Saviour looked small to me, and my heart would not relent. I could not feel that I had been the chief of sinners. I felt indeed guilty for a few instances of inadvertent falsehood, and realized in some degree their desert, but no repentance toward God. I then resolved to pray for repentance, taking encouragement from that passage, which declares Christ exalted to give repentance and remission of sins. This then was the bur-

2

den of my prayer, Lord give me repentance. Still I felt no repentance, and knew I could not come to Christ without it. Thus refuge failed me. Nearly six months passed in this way. I knew there was a door of hope, but could not find it, and was destitute of the qualifications which Christ requires of those who come to him, and was ever likely to remain so. In this situation I was made to feel that it was impossible for me to exercise one holy affection, repentance, faith or love, so completely depraved was I, so helpless, so wretched, and seeing no remedy for my disease, I gave up the object of my prayer, which had been repentance, and committed my case to the great Physician, feeling that however difficult and peculiar it was, it could not baffle his skill. At this moment I felt from a source without myself a reliance upon the faithfulness of God, and great composure, attended with the belief, that he would ere long show himself gracious. This was my feeling when I fell asleep, and this my settled conviction when I awoke. I experienced, however, no particular change afterward. My predominant exercise was reliance upon God. I opened my feelings to but one person, a minister who had preached for us a few Sabbaths, and felt disposed to keep them secret. I enjoyed a peace from time to time to which I think I had been a stranger before, but yet did not dare to hope I was really a Christian, but wanted to enjoy the peace I felt. This state continued till the fall after I was seventeen, when the sentiment expressed in this text, 'He that is not for me is against me, and he that gathereth not with me scattereth abroad," made such an impression on my mind that I felt constrained to put on the Lord Jesus Christ by public profession."

The following extracts from her journal show the general state of her religious feelings at the time of her baptism and subsequently for nearly two years.

"Nov. 1st, 1825.   Thoughts respecting baptism.
2d.   Relinquished.
3d and 4th.   Resumed and continued.
5th.   Attended church meeting, related my religious experience, and was approved as a candidate for baptism.
6th.   Sabbath. — Resolved, if circumstances are favorable, to receive the ordinance.
Noon. — The other candidates decline.   Shall I neglect duty on this account?   Courage.   Duty obscured; tumultuous thoughts; at length conclude to postpone it till another time.   Fearful apprehensions of having erred ensue, with darkness and distress. Attempt to pray, but no access to the throne of grace.   Try to quell my tumultuous thoughts, succeed for a little time.   At tea Elder W. relates some circumstances attending a reformation, particularly respecting baptism.   Now tears, hitherto painfully suppressed, relieve my distracted soul.   In the evening attend prayer meeting; awful solemnity, pensive melancholy, pervades my mind.   Spake a word for God; great relief, consolation, and even animation succeeded.   Returned from meeting, still in a solemn frame.
7th.   Have enjoyed quiet repose, interrupted,

however, by ascending desires. Distress returns. At length become gradually composed, enjoy sweet consolation and delight in reading David, and freedom in prayer. Resolve that I will search the Scriptures, making the Bible my dearest friend and close companion.

9th. Employed in preparing for a funeral. My thoughts solemn, and my resolution to devote myself entirely to God firm.

10th. Last night closed the eyes of a young woman; solemn event! I never before witnessed a death. I hope she is happy. O how thankful ought I to be that my prayers in her behalf are answered. Let me never more distrust the faithfulness of the Saviour. Bless the Lord, O my soul, and forget not all his benefits.

Died at noon, O. H. W. What is his state? Alas, I fear! O that these solemn warnings might prove salutary to surviving mortals. Lord, give me a spirit of prayer, that these events may be sanctified. This evening unable to attend meeting. How much I desire that the Spirit of the Lord be poured out upon those who are assembled and those who are not. Lord, beget a joint cry unto Thee for thy blessed Spirit.

11th. This day attended the funeral of M. C. My mind has been sensibly struck with the awful situation of the people in this place, and with the importance of Christians praying that this death and that of O. H. W. may be blessed to careless sinners.

This afternoon and particularly this evening I may regard as favored seasons. For what, earthly, would

I exchange these joys? My God, continue and increase them; let not this ardor for thy cause, and intense desire for a revival, abate, till I shall see the utmost accomplishment of my wishes. O Lord, give us a spirit of prayer, and grant that the prayers of all thy saints may unitedly ascend to Thee as acceptable incense, and produce a quick return."

In the following paragraph, written at this time, may be seen the strength and ardor of pious feeling which characterized the whole of her public life.

"My Christian friends, are souls for whom Christ died, of so little consequence as not to call earnestly for our exertions? O remember he who converteth a sinner from the error of his way shall save a soul from death. If ye be unconcerned, where is your likeness to Christ? Remember he has enjoined it as a test of love to him to feed his sheep and his lambs. Aged Christians, be not weary in well doing; it is a blessed cause, and now is your salvation nearer than when ye believed. No man having put his hand to the plough, and looking back, is fit for the kingdom of heaven. Perhaps some of my dear friends, who hope in a Saviour, are neglecting to manifest it. Let me ask you why you do so? Are you ashamed of Christ? Remember what he saith of such and tremble. Are you not confident that you are born again? Every sacred obligation binds you, whatever be your state, to glorify God; nothing can justify your backwardness. You rob God of the honor which is his due, and how can you expect to prosper? You have hid your Lord's talent in a napkin in the earth; tremble when you think of our Lord's parable. As you are, and indeed as we all are, how can we be the salt of the earth, and the light of the world, or a city set on a hill if we be thus hid. Be admonished to arise and stand firmly upon the Lord's side. The Lord himself help you thus to do.

14th. At prayer meeting realized the presence of the Lord. My soul has rejoiced in God my Saviour. But amidst all my joy I have cause to lament my own insensibility and impenitence, and to call upon the Lord to give me a sense of the aggravated sinfulness of my heart. O for a broken heart and a contrite spirit.

19th. Last night at meeting had the unspeakable pleasure of welcoming my dear friend E. B. to the blessed cross of Christ and the society of Christians. This, I view, is in answer to prayer. My God, let me not be less thankful than glad, then shall I indeed render Thee unfeigned thanks. Evidences of conviction are beginning to appear in the conduct of many. Lord, perfect thy work, glorify thyself. Some are still stubborn and haughty, O, that they may be brought low by the arrows of the Almighty. Give me a lowly mind and a penitent spirit, let me have such an affecting view of Christ and of my own sinfulness, as will ever make me humble at the feet of Jesus. I long to have it in my power to do something for Christ, that by great vigilance, I may, if possible, redeem the time.

22d. Have just heard that M. B. and A. B. have received comfort. O how shall I express my joy at this intelligence! Happy family, so little while ago proof against everything good, now brought to submit, three of them in eight days, to the mild sceptre of King Jesus. Glory to God in the highest! He has begun a glorious work here, let him reign king of nations as he is king of saints. Great God, carry on tly work till this town, so long given to wickedness, shall universally experience thy love.

Evening. — Have just had an opportunity of witnessing the altered appearance and heavenly countenance of M. B. How tender is her mind, how much like a tender infant, contemplative, calm! A new world is opened to her view, she just breathes the heavenly air, but seems hardly able to move. How necessary that she be fed with the sincere milk of the Word. Lord, help her to grow thereby and strengthen her that she may be bold in thy cause and very useful to her former associates. How much I myself need to be instructed. I am almost ready to conclude I have nothing to do in a public capacity.

24th. Have attended a lecture to the youth. "Rejoice O young man," &c. Felt a deep concern and an uncommon spirit of prayer for the unconverted. O that this solemn call may have an abiding effect on the hearts of many. O Lord let it not be lost, let it be like seed scattered in good ground, which shall in due time spring upward.

29th. My hope is much revived and seasons of doubt and distress begin to disappear. I will look to the Lord, whence cometh my help.

30th. As foul weather always tends to inspire me with melancholy, I have not this day wholly escaped.

My exercises are rather peculiar for me. I never have been apprehensive I should ever be cold and indifferent in the blessed cause of Christ; but this week, such thoughts fill me with distress. Also thoughts almost blasphemous have entered my mind. I have been left for a moment to envy those who have no duty to do, and wished I had none. But, horrid thought! What is this, but to wish I were not a Christian? for a Christian has always a duty to do. I thank God that I soon was able to triumph over those wicked thoughts, and to rejoice that I am counted worthy to suffer in the cause of Christ, and that the goodness of God has enabled me hitherto to take up my cross and follow the Saviour.

Dec. 4th. This day has been one of the most important of my life. I have, in the presence of my fellow men, publicly espoused my Saviour by being baptized. O what a solemn thing! Never did terrestrial things look so to me as at present, never were my reflections so awful. I heartily wish to be entirely devoted to my blessed Redeemer. I do not repent of the sacrifice I have made; no, 'tis a blessed privilege to follow Christ in every institution. I covet to obey every command and imitate every example. I heartily give myself to God to be for him and for none else. I am enabled at times to use the endearing term — My Father — with the greatest satisfaction. But I have never had the peculiar and wonderful manifestations of Deity which many have had; this is a matter of great discouragement to me. I take courage, however, from the words of our Saviour; " Blessed is he that hath not seen, and yet hath believed." I hang upon the word of God. I crave the teachings of his holy spirit. I pray incessantly for inward conformity to Christ, for penitence of soul and for correct views of God. O blessed God, I have solemnly given myself to thee, if thou wilt please to accept me, if thou wilt confer on me the honor of serving thee, I will be thy obedient child.

Never before have my feelings been such as I have experienced this day. In the morning, contemplative, serene; at noon, in view of my baptism, unshaken, deeply impressed with the solemnity of the institution. At prayer by the water side, my request ascended indeed; in singing, I could join, weeping in view of my unworthiness to receive so sacred an ordinance. I had hoped and prayed for some wonderful manifestation of the Saviour at this time, but such I had not. Coming up out of the water I felt a sweet satisfaction in having obeyed the divine command. In the afternoon heard an excellent discourse from these words; "Jesus of Nazareth passeth by." How beautiful; how solemn! At evening, reviewing the discourse of the afternoon, and the transactions of the day rising before me, this question proceeded from my lips and from my heart, What have I done? The answer was, You have presumed to receive a rite which you was not fitted for. I immediately believed it and was hopeless. Distress, awful and severe, seized my soul. I did not retire till after one o'clock, and had I not been interrupted, could not have been willing to do so then without finding relief. For awhile I could not sleep, viewing my soul in infinite hazard. When I awoke my distress returned, no relief. I asked my sister to pray for me, she did, and I felt some more composed, but no satisfactory evidence. I resorted to the Word of God and found the words, 'Thy prayer is heard,' and was enabled to receive them for myself."

She now had an elevated purpose. Though from the moment she was first in her class in the school she attended in Boston, she resolved to act in no medium capacity, though the anticipation of being permitted to fill the first place occupied by her sex, of commanding an influence which would give her power, honor, and preëminence, constantly urged her onward, she had not had a holy aim, now she resolved to consecrate her powers to her Redeemer. She had strength of intellect, energy of character, and a restless desire for constant employment. She thirsted to act efficiently, to act for the cause of God. Teaching was the sphere selected. Though versed only in the elements of an education, and destitute of funds to defray the expenses of an extended course at a literary institution, she does not hesitate. She is immediately resolved what to do, and has that oneness of design, that perseverance in effort, which renders her success certain. Winter district schools would afford a good compensation, and enable her by her own personal exertions, to secure that literary course at a public seminary, which would soon give her the position she desired. She entered upon her design, acquired funds, and soon her name was enrolled as a member of the New Hampton Institution. This was even before the Female Seminary was projected. A small class was admitted at the male department then under the supervision of Rev. B. F. Farnsworth. She attended school till her funds were expended, then resorted to teaching, and again became a pupil. This course she continued until at the age of twenty-one she became principal of the New Hampton Female Seminary, at its commencement in May, 1829. Soon after making a public profession of religion she commenced teaching in Elsworth.

Elsworth, Dec. 18th. Her journal continues: "My mind is deeply impressed with eternal things, and I still feel an anxiety to be engaged in the cause of God, and in some way to promote the interest of immortal souls. I feel that I am entirely dependent upon the Lord for instruction and comfort for myself and for usefulness to others. Jesus is here as well as in Rumney. Let my confidence be entirely in him.

20th. An awful sense of the worth of souls, and the dangerous state of the unconverted, rests upon my mind. I feel a great desire that the Lord would come here by his spirit, but fear if he should make me an instrument of good I should be vain. O for humility, for lowliness of mind, for more of the blessed spirit of God to pervade my heart. I pray, but so faithless; not in the name of Christ I fear. Oh how sin has polluted my soul. Lord grant me quickening and renovating grace, employ me in thy work and glorify thyself. I feel great diffidence with regard to governing my school properly. O for divine assistance. 'Tis a consolation that I have prayers for my success. I feel my dependence to be alone upon the Almighty.

25th. Sabbath. I have reason this day to render thanks to the Lord for his kind protection during the last week, and that he has prospered me in my school. O that he would still lend his aid, and make me still feel my dependence upon him for support. I do not enjoy the sensible presence of the holy spirit as I wish, but am resolved to persevere in the way of holiness and to apply constantly to the great fountain head of blessings. I am encouraged to ask for the Holy Spirit, for the Lord has himself promised, ' All who ask shall receive.' Blessed Spirit, if I have thee, I have enough.

Jan. 1st, 1826. My soul! how swiftly do thy years roll on. Soon the clods of the valley will cover me; soon my years will be numbered and I among the dead. My soul, what resolution hast thou to make for the present year; what retrospect of the past hast thou taken! O for the guidance and teachings of the Holy Spirit. *I resolve to endeavor to live nearer my God and to be more active in the cause of his Son.* God has, this day, removed in some degree his sensible presence, but I must betake myself more earnestly to prayer, and hope for the return of his blessed favor. O God, I cannot pray to thee in an acceptable manner, unless thy Holy Spirit indite my petitions for me, but I can say, " Draw me and I will run after thee. Search me and see if there be any wicked way in me, and lead me in the way everlasting."

> ' Dear Lord, I give myself away,
>   'Tis all that I can do.'

10th. Doubts about my situation, pride and vanity possess my heart. I hardly dare approach the mercy-seat. God my helper has lent me aid to-day, for which I ought to give thanks, but oh what poor returns do I make for all his kindnesses. I say this in view of having attempted to pray, while I found my heart far off from God, and detected myself in rendering .him lip service.

29th. The past week, spent with my friends in Rumney, has been one of the most interesting of my life. On the Sabbath, heard an excellent sermon by Rev. Mr. Blanchard, from these words, ' Is there no balm in Gilead? Is there no physician there?' My mind, amidst deep despondency, received a ray of hope that mercy is not forever gone, and that however mysterious and singular my standing is, it cannot baffle the skill of our great Physician. I determined to seek for an interest in Christ with unabated zeal, until he appear for my help. I thought it would be a privilege to ask the prayers of Christians, but feared they would not pray aright, if I should. How shocking the consideration that I had deceived them! how much I dreaded a disclosure, yet expected one day it must take place. These melancholy meditations I continued to indulge, and determined to give up my hope. Thursday morning had some conversation with Deacon B. relative to my peculiar state;

vented my grief in tears; and poured out my sorrowful soul with plaintive strains into the bosom of my compassionate Saviour. Found some relief, and before night gained considerable strength. Before my return to this place, enjoyed several most delightful interviews with Christian friends, the memory of which is still sweet to my soul. O may I, in resuming the duties of my school, enjoy the divine blessing.

Sabbath evening, Feb. 5th. — Have reason to be thankful that I am still in a land of hope, and that God's mercy has followed me this week. I have received blessings especially in devotional exercises in school. The state of my mind has this week been comparatively peaceful. Have been much in prayer, and felt an entire dedication of myself to God. I wish the will of God may be manifest with regard to my future destiny, that he would count me worthy to suffer for his sake, and that he would discover to me my own sinful heart, and give me true repentance and godly sorrow; that he would make me humble at his feet, and assign me the lowest place in his service. I am astonished at my stupidity, and that I am still doubtful respecting my having passed a renovating change. Unbelief and self-complacency haunt and distress me. O that the eyes of my understanding might be opened, that I might be brought to weep bitterly in view of my situation. Now when the most important events are transpiring both in regard to myself and the cause of Christ, how unmoved am I; how prayerless, or rather how cold are my prayers, which ought to be incessant and fervent. Lord forgive my coldness, and inspire me with zeal and a spirit of prayer.

Feb. 12th. The past week, have been too stupid. 'My drowsy powers, why sleep ye so,' may well be adopted by me. I have visited the throne of grace too little, and in consequence of self-sufficiency have been left to try my own strength, left to my own folly; just is the punishment, I acknowledge. How sinful I am! how deeply is the infusion of corruption fixed! O that I might be favored with only the crumbs from my master's table.

March 5th. The past week, have enjoyed a remarkably peaceful frame of mind. The first of the week I was too stupid, but I looked to the Lord, whence cometh my help. I trust he appeared for me in applying to me some consoling passages of Scripture. I believe I have felt a little increase of faith; O for an increase of all the graces of the Spirit.

March 15th. Received news that my brother lies at the point of death. O Lord, grant us a parting evidence that he sleeps in Jesus, and we give him up.

18th. My brother is dead. Silencing complaints and restraining grief, I am enabled to preserve considerable composure. But little interest, however, at the throne of grace, my mouth seems shut, while I adore and tremble. 'Tis hard to think God chastises in love, certainly he *seems to frown*. How ignorant and short-sighted am I. O my God, sweetly mould my will to thine. I can say little else than, 'Lord sanctify afflictions.'

On the day of her brother's funeral she says —
" My mind is entirely enwrapped in melancholy con-
templations, except when a ray of joy arises from a
hope of happiness complete beyond the grave. Let
me take the admonition to ' be also ready.' I feel
as if I ought to make it the main business of my life,
to make my calling and my election sure. I am
afraid I am deceived. How shall I determine !
Great God, who knowest, assist me to understand.
May my peace be made with thee that I may be
ready to depart. I am almost ready to give up my
hope, but in my distress, the thought that there is
still forgiveness with God, that he promises to hear
prayer and that I am still on praying ground, gives
me relief. Then I repair to the throne of grace, but
fear I am hoping in the mercy of God without any
application of it ; thus does my hope waver. Poor
frail mortal that I am, of all, the most strange and
inconsistent. My God, I must throw myself on thy
mercy, and hope for deliverance.

April 1st. My eyes are blessed with a delightful
view of returning spring, and the powers of my mind,
which have been for a long time absorbed in melancholy contemplation and fearful thought, begin to
possess their natural cheerfulness, and to take some
interest in passing scenes and future prospects. I
desire to possess vivacity and cheerfulness, yet in
this state I shall find it necessary to maintain a
double guard against worldly-mindedness. God has
blessed me once more with a comfortable hope. I
have had a view, peculiar for me, of the all-sufficiency
of Christ Jesus to supply every lack of grace in my

soul, and of his office-work as Mediator. He appears to me a rock indeed, firm, immovable, and a sufficient portion for me. I have some fears still that I may fall upon this rock and be broken, instead of having my goings established thereupon. I have likewise realized how completely condemned by the law of God I am, and the justice of the condemnation. For this I desire to return unfeigned thanks; it is what I have most desired and what I still desire in a greater degree. I am now perusing Doddridge's Rise and Progress of Religion in the Soul. This book gives me more encouragement than any other that I have read except the Bible. But I find my heart too little susceptible of tender emotions; it has too little sense of sin and too little grief on account of it; this is the ground of all my doubting. May I be more alive to the things of Christ, more dead to the world, and attain to some resemblance of my perfect example, and feel that union with Christ which he prayed the Father for just before his ascension.

April 13th. Summer seems to appear to-day, but for me it has lost its charms. The buzzing of the flies announce their joyful liberation, but to me it is a melancholy sound. They bring so fresh to my mind the times when all was gaiety and lightness of heart, and discover the dreadful contrast in such a manner, that every breath is pensiveness and melancholy. Oh death! what a change has thy sad visit wrought! He who was formerly companion with me of spring, and whose heart so lately beat high with hope, sleeps in the cold earth! My brother, so dear to me, so familiar to my sight, I almost imagine

3*

thee here! Can it be that those eyes are for ever closed in death, that thou art no longer sensible of anything that passes? A mother's grief moves thee not! Thy sisters, broken-hearted, with bitter anguish, call thee again and again, but no answer from thy clay-cold lips! No expression in thy eye, no extended arm, attended with the effusions of a heart always so joyful to behold our countenances! Though the grave has become thy home, and thou hast no part with the living, the silken cord of brotherhood still clings to the heart of thy bereaved sister! The scenes in which thou so lately hadst a part, rush into my mind, bringing solemn admonitions! Must I alas run on till suddenly laid aside by thee to wait the end of all earthly things? Merciful God, sanctify afflictions. Hitherto thou hast visited us in mercy, and we profited not; just is thy afflicting rod; but O, by it make us but obedient children and then we will rejoice in thee.

April 15th. Tomorrow's dawn will usher in another precious Sabbath; precious, because it is the day on which my Saviour rose, and precious, because I hope to meet him with his saints. How much I long to be in his sweet presence, to feel the operation of the Comforter, to feel my union to him, perfect and strong as his, with his Father. But I mourn a corrupt nature. O, how glad would I be, according to Bunyan's beautiful representation, to leave all pollution in the river Death, and ascend the banks, prepared to enter the celestial city! My heart bounds at the thought!

May 6th. To-day has been a time long to be remembered by me. In the morning a cloud seemed to overspread my sky. I had for a long time looked with expectation and desire towards this solemn day. In view of the sacred ordinance of the Lord's Supper, I felt a deep sense of unworthiness, and my constant prayer was, Prepare my heart, O Lord, for the solemn scene. It is the first time that I have ever received the symbols of our Saviour's body and blood, a memorial of his dying love. O, what can be more affecting, what more impressive! This day I most cheerfully renew my covenant with the God of heaven, earnestly desiring that I may be enabled to rise to newness of life, to travel towards perfection, hoping to attain unto the end of my race with joy.

7th. This day has been one of my favored seasons. I have seemed freely to commune with my Maker and Redeemer. Glorious privilege; how unmerited! But I dread the time when I shall again mingle, heart as well as hands, in the low concerns of time. O, when shall I be done with these things and be enabled to praise God with an undivided heart!

21st. To-day has been a refreshing time. The gospel has been preached in faithfulness, and has been exceedingly precious to my soul. A revival is commencing, I hear, in H*****. Bless the Lord, O my soul. I feel as if it were in answer to prayer. It is a day of joyful tidings; the Lord visits his vines with showers of divine grace. His kingdom comes; O 'tis the joy of my heart. Miss C. seems perfectly happy. I am not humble enough to receive such abundant consolation. But I ought to be thankful for the happiness I do enjoy; my mind being at present comparatively free from anxious doubt about my spiritual state. One painful thing I know, that I am proud, worldly-minded, carnal, apt to depart from the living God.

June 4th. The state of religion is increasingly interesting; but O, how little do I feel for others' woes! How little do I plead with the Saviour of sinners to attend the means of grace with the sword of the Spirit! How little thankful am I for the special tokens of his favor to me; for that sweet, indescribable peace of mind which I sometimes enjoy! How can I be satisfied when I wrestle with God so feebly! O, that I might cry fervently day and night for Zion's prosperity. My attention is too much diverted; how I wish I were entirely devoted to the Redeemer's cause. Lord let me lift one prayer to thee. I am thine, O keep me thyself, and fit me for thy work, let me be disentangled from things earthly, and let my ultimate design and present incentives to action be thy glory, and the spread of the blessed gospel of salvation.

18th. I have reason to praise God in the highest strains for the blessings of this Sabbath morning. The glorious sun shines in full splendor, all nature rejoices, and the incense of devotion arises from humble and contrite hearts to the Giver of all good things.

Evening. My feelings to-day have been remarkably excited by a consideration of the unspeakable blessedness which awaits the true followers of Christ. I have been greatly blessed in hearing the gospel. Truth so glorious could not fail to fill my soul with joy. My feelings never were before precisely as they have been to day. But I know they will be transitory, because they arise more from a view of the unspeakable blessedness of a religious course, in this world and that to come, than from a sense of the peculiar excellences and glories of the Godhead ; though I would hope, the knowledge of this truth is, in my mind, connected with the happiness of the true disciples of Christ. Wonders so overpower my senses at this time, that I am hardly capable of writing; methinks I almost hear the music of the upper world. But I want to feel more humble, more penitent, more constant in my exertions for the glory of God, and the up-building of his kingdom. I cannot say, more swallowed up in divine meditations, or more transported, but more meek, more sensible of the sufferings of the Saviour, and clearer, calmer and more steady views of him. O that I may be guided, protected, blessed, taught and disposed of to his glory.

19th. My soul is ready to die within me, when I think of my unaccountable distance from God. How unworthy in his sight must be all my offerings, while I have so little sense of his attributes. Let a view of thy majesty and glory O Lord, fill my mind, and awaken therein the deepest self-abasement. My heart is hard, but let me not distrust thee. Forbid unbelieving thoughts; thy grace is sufficient for me, though my malady be incurable from every other source. There is balm in Gilead and a skilful physician there. I will hope in the mercy of the Lord.

20th. Everything conspires to call forth my gratitude and praise.

July 2d. The sermon this morning led to deep self-examination; my hope wavered and my spirits were depressed. By noon my mind was completely perturbated, no clearness of thought, not the least composure, and in view of the Lord's Supper, awfully solemn. I however ventured forward, and enjoy more serenity of mind, but not the sweet sensibility to all the affecting considerations claiming attention in the commemoration of our Saviour's death.

6th. My mind is called particularly to consider how fleeting is time! What memorial do my days leave behind them; how little is accomplished by my busy engagements! O that I may so number my days as to apply my heart unto wisdom.

16th. Followed to the grave one of my scholars. Trust I have been in some degree faithful to her, but not sufficiently so; my exertions have not been unremitted; I feel the importance of greater zeal for the salvation of my fellow creatures while there is an opportunity.

18th. At conference meeting one remarked that we are the Lord's and have no right to plan as if we were our own. I felt the full force of the remark, and was reminded of my former resolutions. I would now solemnly, as in the presence of God, invoking his strength and protection, renew my covenant with him to make his glory my first object, and to proceed in no concerns without reference to his will. I resolve that the first exercise of my mind, if possible, in the morning, but certainly, the first exercise of the tongue, shall be an offering to the Lord, and a request for his blessing. May the Lord ever enable me so to

live as daily to renew my spiritual strength, and honor
the cause I have espoused.

My days are numbered and fast accomplishing.
Every evening seals up an account for itself. O my
God! forgive my criminal insensibility and quicken
me. Do enable me to perform the work which remains to be done by me, before the night of death
seals up my final account. Never before did I seem
so vile. O for the quickening influences of the Holy
Spirit.

27th.

> ' What shall I render to my God
> For all his kindness shown ? '

At conference meeting this evening, I was, I trust,
made joyful in the Lord; I could say 'My soul doth
magnify the Lord and my spirit doth rejoice in God
my Saviour.' My joys, however, have been rather
ecstatic than of a permanent nature. Miss S. C. related her experience; I felt the fullest evidence of her
conversion and with her a most cordial union of spirit.
Do the angels of God rejoice, and why may not I?
I will praise the Lord and be thankful. Bless the
Lord, O my soul. S. is free, is hearty, is humble;
she may be, with the greatest propriety, termed a
young convert: sweet sound. I feel a peculiar interest for those who are uneasy and inquiring the way
to Zion, but have not a full sense of their miserable
condition, nor of the loveliness of the Saviour. I was
in this situation so long, I have tasted the wormwood
and the gall, and my soul is drawn forth in pity for
them.

30th. What account can I give of the improve-

ment of the holy Sabbath. I find that I have hitherto lived too much to myself. My desire is now,
that I may yield myself a servant of God. My mind
has been very wandering to-day, or at least vain
thoughts have frequently intruded. O for strength
to conquer this propensity of my mind. My enemies, the foes I have within, are too strong for me
without divine aid. O how many griefs do they
cause me? when shall I come off victorious? Dear
Saviour, assist me by thy grace and I shall conquer.
My hope sometimes looks not quite right to me. I
desire to be assisted to examine myself by the strict
rule of the Word of God. I resolve as far as practicable to arise an hour earlier than usual for the purpose of meditation and prayer. May the God of
grace assist me in future to live in his service,
and to grow in grace, and in the knowledge of the
gospel.

Aug. 9th. The clock strikes another hour out of
existence. 'Tis past eleven, but how can I sleep
away these precious moments. I have been contemplating the shortness of human life, and glancing
at the emptiness to me of time which is past. I feel
more deeply than ever the importance of diligence;
but I still feel my own weakness and entire dependence on God for energy and unabated zeal in his
cause. I have had this evening great satisfaction in
prayer and an unusual solemnity pervades my mind.
Enveloped in shades of night, while all the family
suppose me reclining upon my bed, I feel it a privilege in this silent way, to give vent to the feelings of
my burdened spirit. My God knows every com-

plaint and every desire. Have been reading the life of Newton; very often is the ground of my hope tested; it is now again to be examined to see if it will stand the trial of the great day. My Saviour is still on his mercy seat, and my day of probation is continued. If pardon never has been granted me, oh that it may now be bestowed according to the riches of his grace.

17th. My mind seems given up to vanity in reference to things which should awaken only gratitude. I made some exertions to prevent it, but was overcome. I forgot to use the weapon of prayer. I now resolve, whenever temptations assail me, to flee to the armory of God. May he help me and with the temptation, find a way for my escape."

About this time she enters upon a course of study at the New Hampton Institution, under the tuition of Rev. B. F. Farnsworth. Her journal continues.

" New Hampton, Sept. 10th. How swiftly, one after another, do Sabbaths come and go! Precious moments! This morning I have had a precious season in prayer; I can include in my supplication the large extent of the whole universe; India is not too far off to be recollected; nor my dear friends in Burmah, surrounded by the horrors of war, perhaps imprisoned. Dear friends! How much they are willing to suffer for the sake of Jesus! I trust all their privations are made up to them by the presence of their dear Redeemer. I long to be engaged for the glory of God and the good of immortal souls.

4

But why not more faithful over a few things, if I would wish to be made ruler over many things? O for strength from above, for divine energy! My grateful heart would rise in thanksgiving to God for his manifold blessings to me as an individual, and to his churches in my day. Often has the burden of my prayer been, O Lord make me love thee, change my heart, take away this heart of stone, and give me a heart of flesh. I ask no other token that Heaven will be mine, than to be sure that I love thee. Now I trust my soul goes out in fervent prayer, and if not deceived, I can say with a full heart, 'Thou art the guide of my youth and my portion forever.' Let the Lord be praised, it is his doing and glorious in our eyes. His long languishing and mourning churches have been visited with showers of grace, and mine eyes have seen his salvation. 'O give thanks unto the Lord, for he is good, for his mercy endureth forever.' The gospel to-day has been a blessing to my soul; trust I felt the warming influences of the divine spirit, the witness within to the truth of the gospel, the believing of it with the heart. How precious is the name of Jesus. I love to hear it extolled; surely it is above every name. I would give him the full possession of my heart, and dedicate myself entirely to his service.

Oct. 1st. By the preaching of the gospel to-day my mind has been rendered somewhat solemn, but I mourn that I cannot feel more, that my heart is not broken, and mine eyes flowing with contrition. My heart is hard, my affections cold, and my joys suspended. I will look to the Lord, I will cry unto him for the influence of his grace to quicken me, and for a view of his lovely face to cheer me. My faith is weak, my love cold, pride oppresses me, envy dwells in my bosom, ambition fills my heart, and I can hardly help exclaiming, I shall one day fall by the hands of mine enemies; but I trust, the Lord, who has often been my helper, will again appear for me. The sermon to-day from the following words, 'Come unto me all ye that labor and are heavy laden, and I will give you rest,' has led me again to question the reality of my adoption as a child of God. I fear I never saw the nature of sin so as to be heavy laden under it. Thick darkness surrounds me, my case is singular, but I do rejoice that it cannot baffle the skill of the great Physician. I trust there is still balm in Gilead. Though my Saviour hides his face I remember him still, and hope for deliverance.

8th. Situated as I am, my opportunities for secret prayer are unfavorable; this is a great loss to me. The habit of neglect grows strong by indulgence, and while I am thus being rendered defenceless, the inward foes to my peace arise and rule. I am seeking knowledge, but alas knowledge puffeth up; spiritual pride is now a formidable foe on the one hand, and slothfulness on the other. Lord, teach me faithfully to improve the advantages thou hast given me, and to improve them from right motives. Among the acquisitions of knowledge which I so much value, may I attain the wisdom to know myself as the chief of sinners, and Christ as my great, all-sufficient Saviour. The word of God seems very precious. How frequently does the prophecy of Isaiah, the subject of my reading and meditation this morning, advert to the coming of the Messiah! The least glimpse of him that appears in the prophets my soul catches with eagerness. I love to dwell upon his name. The sweet Psalmist of Israel has refreshed me this afternoon. How invaluable is the treasure which the Bible contains. It is able to make me wise unto salvation; well may I prize it.

15th. My morning exercise in reading the Scripture was very comforting. In hearing the gospel preached to-day, my heart seemed to burn within me. The things of Christ, which the gospel declares unto us, should ever cause the Christian's heart to leap for joy.

22d. This morning enjoyed a comfortable season in prayer. Truly delightful instruction and entertainment was also afforded me in reading and studying the Acts of the Apostles. Yet I have to lament, how few of my thoughts centre upon that dear object of my adoration, the precious Saviour.

Nov. 19th. This day I may well record as one particularly favored of the Lord. I have enjoyed a great privilege in setting at his table with his saints, and commemorating his death and sufferings.

Dec. 10th. Last Monday was the anniversary of my baptism, and I trust I felt in some degree a desire to renew my covenant with God, which I made when I received that precious ordinance. The thing which I then so little feared, viz. a decline in my religious feelings, alas, has, I fear, to an alarming extent, fallen upon me. But since I have not entirely forgot the law of the Lord, it is my cry that He may restore his wandering sheep. Unless some extraordinary means are used to arouse me, my mind seems now almost entirely engrossed in worldly concerns. Whereas a year ago, almost everything except that which is heavenly seemed excluded. Then I could meditate upon my Saviour in the night season, and when I awoke I was still with Him. But now my mind wanders to the end of the earth. Then the Scriptures were my daily meditation, and searching them my daily, delightful business. Now it is with difficulty that my thoughts are chained to divine contemplation. But still I hope, and at times, if not deceived, enjoy peace in believing.

Dec. 17th. My feelings are so dull, I seem to take but little true enjoyment. When I dedicated myself unreservedly to God about a year ago, I little thought I should ever be thus. I felt then as if I had a work to do, but now I am doing nothing for God, I am living to myself, and in so doing lose all true enjoyment. O that the Lord would in mercy return, and teach me how to live to his glory, and prepare me to die as his servant.

31st. My soul has been moved and encouraged this day, by the preaching of the gospel, to apply once more for a fresh anointing of his Holy Spirit.

Jan. 7, 1827. I have indeed commenced a new year; the past is enrolled in eternity, and will never again be present, till its accounts are all laid open to an assembled world. I write this solemn truth but do I really believe it? How little, alas, does it affect me! I have, indeed, in a poor cold manner, which

4*

seems almost like mockery, endeavored to dedicate myself anew to God, and to pray that I may be led by his spirit. I feel that I am perfect weakness, and notwithstanding this conviction, I am prone to rely upon my own strength.

The sermon to-day adverted to the state of religion at the several missionary stations, and in a most lively manner, exhorted Christians to constant activity. Under its influence my spiritual state appeared in such a light as to dispel the burden of disappointment in my temporal concerns. I hope I shall now be able, with Christian fortitude, to rise above this trial, and regard it as a righteous chastisement of my Heavenly Father, and pray that it may be abundantly sanctified for my good. I feel even now that I can kiss the rod, and bless Him who hath appointed it. 'He wounds to heal; afflicts, to bless.'"

Miss H., at this time, returns to Rumney.

"Rumney, March —. Several weeks have elapsed since I have had sufficient energy to record the exercises of my mind. I begin to feel what a dreadful state of languor I have fallen into, and to examine my situation, and resolve upon a different course. My devotions at the house of God have been so heartless, I determine to devote this day to reading, meditation, and prayer. I find my spiritual affections have lamentably decayed, and I have reason to fear that I am greatly hardened through the deceitfulness of sin. My whole course, since I professed religion, seems to have been tainted by hypocrisy, presumption, or misguided zeal. My duties have been prompted rather by the monitions of conscience, than by any principle of love to God. I seem now, as might be expected of a hypocrite, to be tired thus early in the race, and insensibly drawing my neck from the yoke. I know not what will be my end. I know I am base, altogether corrupt, having a stubborn, rebellious heart, harder than adamant. I fear that I am in the broad road to death, gliding unconsciously down to ruin. Now that I am once more called to arise and trim my lamp, I am determined, if there be any life in me, to attend vigorously to the call. May the Lord break my heart in pieces, that waters may burst forth, that I may not be left to lie down in despair, but may yet praise God in the land of the living.

Monday Morning, April 1st. Lord save me, or I perish. This morning I have prayed to the Lord that he would show forth his power in redeeming me, if I am a wanderer, or in mercy to convict me, if I am a stranger to grace. I have formed some resolutions which I hope to keep, viz.: To exercise more patience ; Not to be easily provoked ; To cultivate filial tenderness ; To strive as much as possible to elude temptation ; To practise every Christian virtue, maintaining strict watchfulness over my deeds, words and thoughts ; endeavoring to be diligent in business, fervent in spirit, serving the Lord. May the Lord enable me to live so as to maintain a uniformly progressive course in the divine life by 'adding to my faith, virtue ; to virtue, knowledge,' &c.

Sabbath Eve. Monday and Tuesday last I enjoyed some foretastes, I hope, of the blessedness of the upper world, some faint, yet most pleasant glimpses of the countenance of my God. During the past week, the Lord has, in a good degree, preserved me from the sins against which I particularly resolved. But I am so harassed with vain thoughts that I have cause to groan aloud. God has expressly declared, 'I hate vain thoughts.' O that he may deliver me from their power.

Sabbath Eve. My resolutions are weak, and sin prevails. I fear that notwithstanding I have put my hand to the plough, I shall be suffered to draw back. My duties are performed hastily and with little interest. I deserve to be an outcast forever from the mercy of God.

Monday Morning. I resolve this morning that with the assistance of God I will maintain constant watchfulness, and will not be neglectful in prayer, nor hasty in the performance of my sacred duties. I resolve to endeavor to burst the shackles, which the vile adversary, in league with my own wicked heart, has fastened upon me. The Lord in mercy will break the net, and let the captive once more go free. May he do it for his mercy's sake.

Sabbath Evening. I have been reading the last part of 'Flavel on Keeping the Heart.' I know my heart has been dreadfully neglected, and with divine assistance I have resolved to heed the expostulation of the pious author, 'to keep my heart with all diligence.' I am so sensible of my own weakness that I hesitate to make any resolves, but I may trust in the aid of Almighty God. I pray that Jesus may be my surety for good, and thus am I encouraged. O may I be wholly sanctified and afterwards received to glory.

May 19th. My birth-day has again returned. Another year is locked up in eternity. Solemn thought ! This day ushers in my twentieth year. It is easy to retrace the time that has fled, but what has it left behind ? This life, which I have so often dedicated to God, what does it present upon a retrospect ? I have this night, before the same altar which I consecrated a year ago, renewed my covenant with my God in a most solemn and unreserved manner. I think, if I know my own heart, I desire to be the Lord's for time and eternity, to be disposed of at his pleasure, and fashioned after his image."

Here the journal of Miss Hazeltine's religious feelings closes. The reason for its discontinuance, as she has often said, was the deep and painful dissatisfaction that she felt with herself. Her performance of religious duties seemed so imperfect, the sins of her nature so little subdued, and her attainments in experimental and practical piety so small, that the record of her feelings became a matter of sorrow and discouragement rather than of confidence and joy. But though she ceased to record her exercises, she did not cease to carry her case to the Lord in fervent, struggling prayer. She knew a true record would be kept in heaven. What shall it be ? was, with her, a question of so much importance that the records of earth appeared, by comparison, unworthy of a thought.

In the preceding narrative I think the reader will have perceived a definiteness,- variety, depth and strength of religious experience, not very common to young ladies of her age. In view of her subsequent history, it is not difficult to perceive the wisdom and goodness of God in making her thus early acquainted with herself as a sinner and with the means of salvation, suited to every variety of spiritual condition. Thus prepared, in no common degree, by her own experience, she enters, two years subsequent to the close of her journal, upon her labors as Principal of the Female Seminary at New Hampton.

CHAPTER III.

An important condition of usefulness was now secured, — a sphere of action. But it was one which
required great energy, and concentration of purpose.
These she had at command. She had learned to
originate her own plans, to anticipate the elements
for a result, and, independently, to give herself to
their attainment. She had simply a house in which
to teach, convenient indeed, but not especially attractive by its size or location ; there were no funds,
no established reputation ; and there were no resi-
dents in the village on whom Miss H. had any claims
from their relation to the Seminary.

She says, in a letter to her mother, at this period,
"I have experienced many vicissitudes of fortune,
have fallen into many errors, escaped many ills, enjoyed many comforts. I have experienced disappointments, mortification and bitter regrets, as well
as the gratification of desire, preferment and pleasure. You have marked, with a mother's tenderness,
my steps. You now see me moving in a respectable
circle, perhaps at the pinnacle of honor. You, my
friends, the world, expect, have a right to expect

consistency and propriety in my conduct, and will no longer extenuate my faults by alluding to my youth. I feel that my judgment will be taxed, my discretion canvassed, my intellect, and the soundness and extent of my education subjects of remark. My talents for communication will be tested, my firmness and virtue tried, my energy and perseverance called into action. O can I stand the trial? My capacities are limited, and my weakness will appear, unless that same Divine Hand which has led me hitherto, be still extended for my aid. O! mother, solicit this aid for me, call down his blessing on your unworthy daughter!"

The first term that the Female Seminary was opened at New Hampton, there were only seventeen pupils, and these comparatively little advanced in the course of education. But no matter. Then was the time to establish the character of the school, which was subsequently, as her ardent temperament predicted, to have no equal. She and Miss Rebecca Hadley, now Mrs. Purkett, of Boston, labored incessantly for these seventeen pupils, and at the close of the summer term the examination proved that the Seminary was conducted by no common mind.

The school immediately became known abroad. Scholars from all parts of New England were enrolled on the list of names. The second term there were more than fifty members, and that with no other inducement than the privilege of hard study.

But a difficulty immediately presented itself. She must be supported, and that too in a manner not to infringe upon her dignity. With all her exertions, she had become somewhat involved in prosecuting her studies, and her present position was far from affording her an ample salary. She says, in a letter to her sister, "I cannot replenish my wardrobe as I would. You know I was obliged to anticipate my salary, and this is very limited. I do not know what to do this winter. I do not think it will do very well, as it concerns my name, to engage in a district school, and besides, I do not know how to spend the time. It will not do for me to engage here in future at this rate for six months. I have thought considerable of going to Virginia. I shall have an opportunity, about a year from this time, to go in company with some of my acquaintances. If suitable encouragement should be given, do you think it would be advisable ?

"Dear Sister, I shall not wonder if you are quite out of patience by this time with my unwarrantable ambition and insufferable egotism. Pardon me, I have no one on whom to lean, alone and unsustained, I will lean on Providence, and may Heaven be propitious. I ought to feel the deepest gratitude for the distinguished mercy which has attended me, yet, my dependence does not supersede the use of means to make the most of the gifts of nature."

Love for the school, the great opportunity to do good, and the evident smiles of Providence determined her still to prosecute her labors at New Hampton. Although her reward in money was small, she received souls for her hire to become stars in her crown of glory. This term there was an interesting revival of religion. Yes, this first fall term, a term which has ever since been so signally blessed by the outpourings of the Spirit of God, was rendered memorable to many hearts, as the season of their spiritual birth. Miss Hadley, Miss Hazeltine's associate, was one of the subjects of this revival. When she returned home at the close of the term, Miss H. wrote the following to Mrs. Hadley:

"DEAR SISTER — I must congratulate you on the happiness which all your little circle with yourself must experience in receiving Rebecca once more, especially as you receive her, I hope, not as you parted with her. She has caused us not a little joy. She has been bold for Jesus; may she continue faithful unto death. I hope you will be quickened by this signal mercy. 'Rejoice evermore, pray without ceasing, in everything give thanks.' May the offering of this Thanksgiving day be sincere from us all, acceptable to God, a sweet smelling savor. I meant to have written to brother H. in this. I know he is ready to say, 'my cup runneth over.'"

Speaking of the subjects of this revival, in a letter to Miss P. P. Rand, she says: "As far as we have heard, all seem to stand fast in the faith. Miss —— suffered persecution from the source she expected, but I believe she bears it with Christian fortitude. Pray for her. Miss —— from M. has written me freely her feelings, and I have tried to direct her in the right path, to influence her to follow the precepts and practices of the early disciples. Some of the converts are to return the following spring. Oh, that we may have wisdom to impart every needed truth.

This second season, to which she refers above, there was no general revival, but a good religious state throughout the year.   In the fall, at the Seminary, and in the winter, at the Institution, there were interesting conversions.   She says, in a letter to Miss C. C. Hall, in the winter of that year, 1831, while a member of the family of Mr. F. : —

"You will be pleased to know that we are enjoying a revival of religion at the Institution.   Miss B., from Boston, Miss L. E. and R. M. have become hopefully subjects of a change of heart.   Time alone will prove to us whether all have passed from death unto life.   Professor F. seems perfectly absorbed in the spiritual interests of the students.   Do not cease to pray for us, and for *me*, who am not worthy the Christian name, that I may feel the influence of the grace of God on my heart, and may live to his glory. I am so much relieved from responsibility, compared with what I have sustained ordinarily, in the charge of scholars, that I am in danger of feeling released from all duty and lying down at ease ; but I am conscious there are no circumstances in the midst of which a Christian may innocently put off his armor, or be off his watch.   I desire to return, without wandering farther, to the Shepherd and Bishop of our souls."

In the summer following, in a letter to Miss Hadley, associate with Miss H., the first and second seasons,

she says, "You are doubtless almost breathless with
expectation, and I hardly know how to tell you what
I would, but can only say, that I hope the Lord is in
this place. There has been an unusual degree of
seriousness upon the minds of many of the young
ladies for about two weeks, and we indulge hope of
three individuals. Some others are still very much
distressed, and others still very thoughtful. I have
never had the solemn privilege of pointing so many,
deeply anxious, to the Saviour as within a fortnight.
They have not seemed as they did last fall, or even
the fall before ; they have seemed to say, 'give me
Christ or I die.' I am all the time trembling lest
some that are anxious should be misled and become
discouraged and go back to their old state, or indulge
hope without reason. It is a fearful time ; you can
realize something of it. The young ladies boarding
with Miss G. have been somewhat thoughtful, but I
do not know as they can be considered as inquirers.
Miss G. is very faithful and much esteemed by all
the young ladies.

"I hope you will not receive the impression from
what I have written, that the excitement is greater
than it is, but you will pray earnestly for us, as I trust
you do, that the Lord will glorify himself by converting many souls here."

CHAPTER IV.

MANNER AS A RELIGIOUS TEACHER.

It was a theory of Miss H. that we cannot hope for a radical change of heart till the mind is enlightened by divine truth ; and to effect this was her constant aim. She read to her pupils the Word of God, not in a formal manner, not because it was an established requisition, but to gather thence truth, rich and varied, which would affect the heart, and influence the life. At the morning devotions, the meeting for social prayer, and in all her recitations, when it could be done with effect, she brought home the truths of religion ; she enforced feelingly, and with evident sincerity, the practical doctrines of Christianity, and her pupils felt that the word spoken was *to* them, and *for* them ; and that they could not hear and be irresponsible.

The school, for several of the first years after it went into operation, was continued only during the summer and autumn. The revival was generally during the fall term. All summer Miss H. sowed the seed, and prayed that her labors might be blessed, both in the presence of her pupils and in the secret chamber, and the silent tear often flowed as proof of

5*

her sincerity. When the fall term was drawing to a close, and the pupils became conscious that they were soon to be deprived of those privileges, there accompanied this consideration the fear that, if they did not then become Christians, their fate might be sealed forever. An earnest seeking for the way of life was the result, and God, faithful to his promise, heard prayer, and was found of those who sought Him with full purpose of heart.

Labor for unconverted souls was the employment which Miss H. most enjoyed. In a letter to Mrs. E., during a winter term, she says, " I almost wish I had my scholars about me as in the summer. All my present pupils but one are pious, and though this circumstance is no reason why I should be stupid, I find much less to prompt me to action than when surrounded by the unconverted. I sometimes ask myself what I should do if I were the wife of a minister ? I seem to feel as if I should try to make the people all Christians, especially those of the parish with which I was connected. It seems now that it would be very different from laboring at my present disadvantage, as I could entirely devote my energies to this one point. The trouble with me is, my attention is divided, and the misfortune of the case is, that the greater share of my interest is given to affairs foreign to religion. It is a miserable way to go by the halves."

In a letter to Rev. Mr. Evans, 1837, during a revival at New Hampton, she writes, " I am sure you will be glad to know that we are having a revival of religion in our midst. It is a very interesting time, Oh, how

can we praise the Lord enough for having visited us
with refreshing showers in the midst of a time of
drought.   We will take the cup of salvation and call
upon the name of the Lord.   Our brethren connected
with the male department have taken hold in good
earnest.   You remember we used to be sorry to have
the good brethren leave, for fear none as *good* would
appear to fill their places.   But I think we never have
had better young men than those now with us.   I
think *very much* of the present theological class.
They are certainly talented and pious."

None but her associates could know, how every
thought, at the time of a revival, was concentrated
upon the salvation of souls.   She then felt her entire
reliance upon God, and in her moments of cessation
from active exertion, she was accustomed to hold
communion with Him, in preparation for the work
then before her, as she, under other circumstances,
communed with books, as a preparation for recitation.
In the night watches, while reposing upon her pillow,
the whispers of prayer could be heard, ascending to
God, for grace and wisdom to win souls to Christ.
In her external plans, in her earnest entreaties, her
efforts and anxiety to secure the prayers and coöperation of Christians in both departments of the institution, it was manifest that her interest was of no
ordinary character.

While she believed that the conscience must be
enlightened by divine truth, before we can hope for
a radical change of heart, she believed in the special
influences of the Spirit.   She felt that when divine
truth had been brought home to the conscience and

heart, then was the time to secure the harvest. She allowed herself and her associates no rest, while there was a manifestation of the special influences of the Spirit. She relied chiefly upon personal conversations, meetings of inquiry, conference and prayer. The subject of religion was then constantly before the mind. The morning exercise was *increasingly* personal, the recitations afforded *unusual* scope for religious instructions, and there were little meetings almost every evening of a devotional character.

Reference has been made, in the letter quoted above, to the assistance of the members of the theological class. These were her reliance out of her own school. The church was so scattered, and its members so little acquainted with the members of the school, that they could render little assistance. But the pious young men caught the spirit of the times, and were efficient co-workers on such occasions.

The history of the religious interests at New Hampton teaches impressively the efficiency of individual Christian fidelity, independent of the public ministrations of the gospel. True, a stated religious meeting, at a stated place, is of inestimable advantage; we can hardly hope to form fixed religious habits without such assistance. But teachers, remote from such aid, need not despair of the converting influences of the Spirit of God. In the Seminary, the entire reliance, in its early history, was upon the Christian efforts of the teachers and pupils. Personal conversation, conference meetings, and meetings for social prayer and inquiry, and Bible-class instruction, were invariably attended with the best results. Indeed, teachers have, in many respects, a decided advantage over a pastor. They have their pupils constantly under their supervision; can know every stage of feeling; can watch the influences brought to bear upon character, and vary these at will. How much is contained in the exhortation, 'Be wise to win souls to Christ!' Miss Hazeltine possessed this wisdom. She read the heart, acquainted herself with the feelings of those around her, and knew the means adapted to effect the best results. How few teachers feel that it is the heart they are to watch and guard; that it is the soul that claims their first, their deepest thought!

CHAPTER V.

We have already seen that Miss H. was at first engaged in teaching only six months in the year, the summer and fall terms. The intervening time was to her a season for prosecuting study, and laying the plans of future labor. Her object was definitely in view, — a school of an elevated order. Every feeling of her soul was interested, and she withheld no effort, nor avoided any responsibility, which could bear upon her purpose. She had been wont to see teachers sleep away the happiest portion of the day, because, forsooth, they were not obliged to labor till nine o'clock. She had seen them while away the whole evening, in fancy needle-work and idle chat, because they could pursue the old track without study or plan. She had known them, for months together, in times of vacation, to fold their hands in sheer idleness. But her habits, her desire for advancement, impelled her to be ever active.

When she commenced at New Hampton, her education was comparatively limited. During her early residence at Boston, she had laid an excellent foundation, by attaining an accurate knowledge of the elementary branches. Under the tuition of Professor Farnsworth, she had prosecuted, to some extent, the study of the Latin language, and examined the common text books upon natural and intellectual science; and, under the instruction of M. and Mme. Bonfils, she had become acquainted with the French language and drawing. Her knowledge of Greek, Hebrew, Italian, political economy, moral science, rhetoric, and biblical and classical literature, for which she was so justly distinguished, was acquired after she became Principal of the Seminary.

Her term of study did not terminate with the commencement of the cares of a teacher. She was always a close student. It was her habit to take up, each term, as many branches of study which required her particular attention, as she gave her pupils, and she did them justice. No one ever had occasion to say, she did not advance as fast and as far as practicable, or that she had not mastered her subject. Her instruction electrified her pupils with a desire to drink deep at the fountain of knowledge. All thirsted for information. And probably the fact, that many of the truths communicated to pupils, were new to the teacher, perhaps acquired by the midnight lamp the night previous, imparted a life to the instruction, which tended to render it much more interesting and effective. She learned with her pupils; but she was their pioneer. She led the

way, pointed out the beauties, laid open the concealed treasures.

She would not have advised others as a matter of
policy, to venture to teach in branches of study with
which they became acquainted only in the progress
of teaching. There are few Miss Hazeltines. There
are few that have her native energy, her willingness
to study, study, *study*, until there is an *assurance*
gained that the subject is fully mastered. Some may
succeed as she did; but it must be at the expense of
sleepless nights, and an anxiety sufficient to undermine the firmest constitution. She had success, notwithstanding these circumstances, and not in consequence of them. But it was at the price of incessant labor.

Miss H. thirsted for every kind of knowledge
which she had not already acquired. In a letter to
a sister she says, " You ask for a comment upon the
study of the languages. I am incompetent to give
it. I studied them through a vain, foolish and criminal desire to hoard up knowledge; which I consider *no better* a principle (except perhaps it has not
quite so degrading an effect) than that which actu-
ates the miser. Still I think them useful. They
afford a strong exercise for the comparing and rea-
soning powers, give a more accurate knowledge of
our own language, and form the habit of confining
the mind closely to any subject, and thus give a sort
of empire over our mental faculties."

She commenced the study of Greek, the winter
after she took charge of the Seminary at New Hamp-

ton, under Professor Farnsworth, and pursued the study more or less during her whole term of teaching. While at Professor F.'s she thus writes to Miss C. H.

"I am now a member of Professor Farnsworth's family, engaged in acquiring something of the Greek language — am very happy as to outward circumstances — making a proficiency quite satisfactory to myself. But I do not know as it will be any blessing to me ; for it has already obtained too great a share of my affections, and too much engrossed my thoughts."

The Hebrew she did not prosecute very far. Two or three years after she commenced teaching at New Hampton, Professor Seixas had a class in Hebrew at Charlestown, Massachusetts. Professor Farnsworth was of the number. It being vacation with Miss H., he wrote her to join Professor S.'s class. She did so, and while there wrote the following to an associate teacher. "My class had advanced one week when I arrived, and I have in consequence had rather less time to be lonesome or to think of you than I expected. I now stand tolerably fair in my class. I have not, however, as I hoped, enjoyed the privilege of reciting with a class of ladies, but am alone among men. You will be surprised, but it seemed rather expedient. Professor F. is present at the recitations, which relieves a little my lonely position. I am rather interested with Hebrew, and hope I shall not regret the sacrifice I have made to acquire it."

For several years after becoming a teacher, it was

her custom to spend, every Spring. several weeks in Boston, for the purpose of prosecuting the study of the modern languages. The following is from a letter written on one of these occasions. " I am under the tuition of Mons. Bonfils, whose Academy is pleasantly located on Mount Vernon street. He was educated in Italy, but has been in America a number of years. He is a gentleman of fine mind, truly scientific, and an excellent instructer. I found my lessons in French very easy, and was induced to commence the Italian language. I am quite delighted with it."

In the prosecution of English studies she needed no teacher. When she commenced examining a new branch of study, for example, Political Economy, or Rhetoric, she bent her energies to the subject. She sought for authors who had most successfully treated it, and made it a topic of conversation, with any one, who could converse understandingly. Thus she kept it before the mind, revolved its various bearings, and digested its leading principles, till she had made herself familiar with the subject, and was ready for a new topic of thought.

She had so completely formed the habit of laboring with a direct object in view, that it was difficult for her to interest herself in a matter that had no immediate bearing upon her course of labor. If she met with a book that illustrated a study she was teaching, she read it with avidity. If it bore upon anything which would be of practical benefit, even at a period a little remote, she would read with interest. But if she could say, what is the use? and reply, none directly, it was with difficulty she could interest herself. She could not endure fictions. Her incessant application to science, after she became teacher in a Ladies' Seminary, gave her little time to devote to literature, and those years when young ladies generally delight in reading anything and everything, when, I had almost said, they drink to intoxication from the fountain of general knowledge, when the ages of the past, with their peculiarities, their excellences, burst upon the astonished vision, she had been confined to the school room, teaching children, and in return, receiving funds to prosecute her own scientific studies. She ever lamented her deficiency of general knowledge, and anticipated with pleasure her release from teaching, because it would afford her more time to read history and poetry, and to become acquainted with the general literature of the past and present.

She was assisted in the prosecution of biblical studies by the theological professors connected with the male department of the institution. As soon as she had decided what portion of Scripture to examine during a given term, she consulted them as to the best manner of investigating the portion selected, and the most approved authors, who had commented on it. She then gave herself vigorously to the study ; and, as she investigated, led on her class. She, of course, had not all that extent of research, that power of criticism, which is possessed by gentlemen teachers of biblical literature. But those portions of Scripture which her class examined, were thoroughly understood. Upon biblical studies she depended for moulding the moral character of her pupils, and in them she secured preëminence. Her instructions from the Bible were the great instrument, in the hand of God, of the many conversions among the pupils of the school, of which she so long had the supervision.

CHAPTER VI.

EXAMPLES OF HER MANNER OF TEACHING.

Miss Hazeltine's knowledge of the Scripture, and of kindred subjects, as will have been anticipated, was more mature than upon any other branch of study. She ever inculcated religious truth, in a most interesting manner. Those who have been her pupils can see her seated at the head of the assembly room. The whole school is before her. She announces, " we will read, this morning, young ladies, the sixth chapter of Hebrews. The Jews, you are aware, were celebrated for imposing forms of worship. Great ceremony and solemnity were preserved in all their holy ordinances. Their great feasts, their solemn fasts, their sacrifices, their chants, the reading of the law, all had a tendency to impress the Jewish nation with a reverence, a holy awe for their religion. And when converts were made from this people to the Christian faith, the perfect simplicity, the entire absence of every imposing form which characterized it, rendered them liable to relapse into Judaism. St. Paul, to prevent this, wrote them an epistle in which he sets forth the respects, in which Christ is superior to the angels, whose ministry they

6*

so much venerated, to Moses their lawgiver, and to
the priesthood who were obliged continually to offer
sacrifices and even for themselves, and thence in-
fers, if neglect of the ministry of angels, the law of
Moses, and the sacrifice of priests, met with merited
punishment, much less would they escape, if they
refused to listen to the teachings of Christ. Let us
notice the instructions given in the chapter before
us."

The chapter is read. The difficult points examined, on which previous assignments had been made.
Then is the application. "My dear pupils, this book
is rich in practical lessons for us. The Jews trusted
in the law — they made their boasts of a holy, devoted life, but all this was of no avail, unless they
listened to the teachings of Christ. And so it is with
you. You may pride yourselves on strength of intellect, exalted virtue, integrity of purpose, and these
are all desirable possessions, but they will be as the
spider's web, if Christ is not your portion. And
why not know the blessedness of calling him yours?
Hear his invitation, 'Ho! every one that thirsteth,
come ye to the waters.' He knocks at the door of
your hearts, till his head is filled with the dew, and
his locks with the drops of the night; O that you
could taste the sweets of religion! that you loved to
sit at Jesus' feet, to receive that instruction, which
none but infinite wisdom can impart. Gladly would
I lead you to the blessed Saviour. Joyfully shall I
bear you in the arms of faith to my Father in Heaven.
I sometimes see you weep, *weep*, I would hope,
because you have not God for your portion; yes,

and though it produces agony to see you sad from any worldly consideration, my heart leaps with joy when I see your bosom swell with penitential grief. Come, my dear friends, to the Saviour ; throw yourselves, with all your imperfections, upon his mercy. The blood of Jesus can remove every stain, cleanse every impurity. Prayer is about to be offered, offered for ourselves, for you. Join in it, and be benefited by it." Silence reigns around. Prayer ascends, prayer that sheds its hallowed influence over the day.

We will enter her recitation room. Miss H. is in the centre, by the table, with the list of the names of her class. The roll is called, and all are present. Moral science is the text book. One gives the topic of the ninth chapter — another a general analysis — a third a particular analysis of the first section, &c. The chapter is recited, the force of the argument impressed, and at the close, the teacher connects it with the preceding chapters and generalizes.

" How appropriately and justly the subject is treated. Two days since we examined the chapter exhibiting the imperfections of natural conscience. It was shown, that we need additional moral light, inasmuch as conscience, unaided by revelation, may fail to teach us all our obligations, or it may fail to teach us in what way to discharge them, or it may not be sufficiently authoritative to counteract contrary impulses. Now our obligations are made manifest by the inspired revelation of the divine will ; the manner of *discharging* them, not only by studying the effect of actions upon ourselves and society, but from direct precept; and we may derive motives, impelling to the performance of duty, by learning from the Scriptures the character of God, in the interesting relations he sustains. Natural religion is defective. This may not tell us all our duty, in its extent and limitations. It may not tell us, sufficiently soon, how to discharge it, or be sufficiently impulsive in its influences, as it can teach only by experience, and certain truths only in advanced stages of society. It can give no facts, nor can it draw motives, except from the present world. In this state of things, it becomes highly probable, that God would make up the deficiency by a direct revelation. The Bible, we have reason to believe, is this revelation. There is certainly great internal evidence, that it is of divine origin. How strong are the motives to virtue, drawn from the present and future world! How tender, soul-stirring, the relations which the Infinite One is made to sustain to us. It would seem that the hardest heart would be impelled by them to a virtuous, holy life."

'Tis the sunset hour, Saturday evening. The ladies of the seminary are assembled in the hall, consecrated to prayer. Silence is broken by the leader of the meeting. "How heavenly, holy, seems this quiet twilight. 'Another six days' work is done.' All care may be forgotten, and for one short hour, we may commune with our Creator, our Preserver, our Benefactor, our Redeemer. We may sing to his praise, in hymns speaking forth the sentiments of our hearts. We may enlarge our desires before him, in addresses at the throne of grace. We may commune with each other — learn to sympathize in each other's disappointments and successes; ah! and best of all, we can ask for the influences of the Holy Spirit, the *Holy Spirit*, which reveals to us the adaptation and depths of the riches and the goodness of the Christian religion, and makes manifest to us our perishing need of just such a provision. That Spirit, which sanctifies our natures, elevates our affections, and brings us near to God, to happiness, and heaven." There is sweet communion with each other, and with God. Prayers have been offered for the forgiveness of the sins of the week — for a sense of the worth of souls, and a readiness to perform every duty. The absent have been remembered, and a preparation for the holy Sabbath, earnestly sought, and the moment for separation is at hand. "We must soon leave this consecrated spot" is uttered, as all rise from prayer. "But there may be some one who would esteem it a privilege to remain, and tell me the emotions of her heart, and pray for a new, and right frame of spirit." The meeting is closed. The many go to their homes. Yet the low voice of warning, admonition and entreaty, may still be heard in the hall of prayer, and perhaps one for the first time bows and prays for the forgiveness of sin and a heart to love God.

The biblical lesson, on Sabbath morning, varied with the class. Sometimes Miss H. acted as president of the Berean Society, sometimes as teacher of the Bible class. She seemed equally fitted for both.

Each member of the Berean, after the opening of the meeting by prayer, was accustomed to present some fact or truth of a religious character. These afforded scope for practical remarks, which tended to enliven, and at the same time, to add solemnity to the feelings. After this, when the Word of God was examined, care was taken to preserve, as far as possible, the feelings of solemnity already awakened. Miss H. did not encourage an inquisitive spirit. She tried to make the lesson practical, and of a devotional character. When she led the Bible class, where all were strangers to God, she attempted rather to impress truths, which would affect the heart, than such as would expand the intellect and feast the reason.

She exhibited by far the most research, in the advanced Bible class, which she was accustomed to instruct daily. Here her powers seemed in full play. She brought forth from the book of inspiration, treasures inexhaustible, priceless. The whole was before us as a map, the Old and the New Testament, the Patriarchal, the Mosaic and the Christian dispensations. She loved to dwell on the last, to present its excellence and its suitableness to our condition, the purity of Christian morals, and the preëminence of their Author. The geography, history, logic and rhetoric of the Scriptures, in turn received her attention. Many who read this, will remember the instructive lessons from her lips, upon the Psalms, Romans, or one of the Prophets, when the recitations have been prolonged for two, and sometimes three hours. While but few teachers were engaged in the Seminary, Miss H. taught whatever branches seemed to demand her attention ; but as soon as an increased number of pupils allowed an increase of teachers, she gave herself principally to the department of biblical literature.

CHAPTER VII.

The character of spiritual guide to her pupils, gave her a strong hold upon their affections. If her efforts resulted in their conversion, this became an inducement to a long course of study, and gave rise to associations, which rendered the position of the pupil at once pleasant and desirable. Before conversion, thirst for knowledge induced them to forego the pleasures of home. Subsequently, the impelling motive was a wish to be prepared to coöperate in the great work of carrying forward the cause of Christ. The school became a spiritual birth-place, which must therefore be ever hallowed with endeared recollections; and its pupils, associates, attached by ties as tender as those of natural relationship.

Next to this, perhaps her success was the result of her power of application. We have already referred to her exertions to meet the incidental wants of the Seminary. Intellectual necessities were not the less energetically considered and supplied. She had a vigorous constitution. Twelve and one o'clock at night found her still at her study-table. This constant application kept her alive to the beauties of intellectual research, so that those who placed themselves under her supervision could not fail to imbibe her spirit. There was always something new to be learned, some glittering mine unexplored, some hidden gems unattained. Every inducement urged her on in the path of research. Her knowledge was definite. She perhaps did not seize a thought as soon as many others; but what she knew, lay before her in all the clearness of a visible representation ; and when she presented her thoughts, she forgot none of those little circumstances, which had a bearing on her own acquisition of the subject.

No one could watch her movements, for a day, and not feel that she was eminently efficient. They saw that if she was engaged in an enterprise, there was no doubt in regard to the issue. This definiteness of view, energy of purpose, and efficiency in execution, constituted a power to use her own acquirements to the best advantage.

She easily perceived the necessary antecedents to any given result, and with her own directing hand could turn the genius, skill and talents of those under her care into the precise channel in which they were best adapted to move. She could use the talents of another as though they were her own, and thus combine powers, the most diverse in character, and never united in the same individual, to promote a single design. A sense of responsibility to God and a desire to secure a consciousness of his approval, united, at the same time, with a desire to deserve and receive the high regard of the wise and good, urged her forward in every noble enterprise. Nothing

7

seemed too laborious, hazardous, or difficult, if by its accomplishment she could render herself acceptable to God or praiseworthy to the esteemed.

She entered into the interests of her pupils, learned their capacities and desires, and made them feel that the interests of each were dear to her heart. She was accessible at all times, and upon all subjects would think and consider for her pupils as for herself, and led them to feel it was her duty and pleasure to be thus interested.

She excelled in teaching her pupils to be wise and good for some practical purpose. Few of them, when asked why they studied, would reply, they did not know. A few months, under her tuition, would teach one to labor for some proposed object, professedly at least a laudable one. She felt, as long as she lived, that teaching was the most desirable occupation in which a young lady could engage, and spared no effort to induce her pupils to enlist in this employment.

Her punctuality contributed much to the interest of the school.

She writes, June 24, 1833: " I am making preparations, this evening, to attend the convention at Rumney tomorrow. It will be the first time I have been absent from my school, except two days by sickness. I feel really solemn. My dear little family seem increasingly affectionate, and very assiduous to do everything to facilitate my leaving. How much you would enjoy this meeting. O how refreshing it is to hear of the progress of the Redeemer's kingdom on earth! Are we not personally interested ?

" We have with us excellent female prayer meetings. I do feel so delighted to see so much of talent and piety among Baptist females of New Hampshire, or certainly of New England, that I can hardly be silent at such times. I do rejoice very much to see them advancing in the paths of literature, science and religion. It is my life." It was her life, and she took occasion to interest her pupils in everything that would bear upon these points. She felt that "noble ends made noble acts." She always kept their powers in exercise, and taught them to render effectual every resource. She taught them to *do* good, as well as to *get* good; and was careful to secure the very time when it could best be carried into effect. On her return from the Convention, she had an opportunity of presenting the various departments of Christian effort. Education was nearest the hearts of her pupils. She could make them feel upon this subject, and lead them to efficient effort.

A little time after the date of the letter above, she writes: "We had an excellent meeting. All the objects of Christian effort, which came before the Convention, were treated in a very interesting manner. I felt, when I came home, that I wanted to do much; and have been endeavoring to do something; but it is uncertain with what effect. The young ladies have acted nobly. On the Monday morning after I returned, they presented me, in the most polite manner, ten dollars to constitute me a life member of the Education Society. It was the more pleasing, as the design originated entirely with themselves.

Miss H. was careful not to dissipate her influence

by dividing her attention. She allowed herself but one absorbing object — her school. It was said of a certain individual, if he had chosen to turn his attention to letters, he might have become as celebrated a scholar, as he was a conqueror, but he might not have become preëminent in both, had he made the attempt. Excellence requires concentration and perseverance. Few excel in many departments at the same time. Miss Hazeltine might have written for the periodicals of the day; she might have had an extensive literary correspondence; she might have allowed her sympathies to have been enlisted in general education, or, in the enterprises of benevolence, which claimed the interest of the community in which she moved; but she knew that one who undertakes everything can do nothing well, and as a consequence, shut out every enterprise but such as her position called her to sustain.

She was judicious in the selection of a class upon which to act. She sought not the wealthy great, or the depressed poor, but the energetic, enterprising, middle class. She says, in a letter to an associate teacher, who was seeking advantages abroad, —

" I am exceedingly glad to hear that you have good society, and that which is refined. Improve all you can, but do not be seduced by appearances. Accomplishments, while they have a real worth, are liable to have their worth overrated, especially, by those who fancy they want them, in their own persons. You know how it has been, in regard to other attainments; they seemed of superlative worth, until acquired; then their value has depreciated. Besides, my love, do not lose sight of the standard, by which God estimates things. We are not to live for our fellow beings alone, that is, for their *applause*, or even for their *approbation*. We *are* to live, for others indeed ; but not in this sense of this phrase. Is it for the accomplished, and *wealthy*, and *polite*, that we are to live ? There is little charity, little virtue in this, methinks. Mrs. More was introduced into refined society, by the providence of God, (the Rev. Mr. Newton thinks) that she might have the opportunity of writing for this class. But I hardly expect this is *our* province ; we must try to benefit ' our fellows. ' "

She had sufficient independence to persevere in whatever was for the interest of the Seminary, though strongly opposed. The year she introduced calisthenics, most of the church; at New Hampton, took a stand against her. But she swerved not from her purpose. She felt that right was on her side, and that the true principle was, to go forward. She says, in a letter to a friend at this time, " I presume I have never been so much the subject of censure, in all my life, as for a few weeks past. I suppose I have been looked upon, by a great many, almost as an apostate. Judge of my feelings. You wish to know what I have done. *They say* I have taught a dancing school. This is my crime. I have known, for some time, that false reports were flying ; but, satisfied of the strict propriety and the entire expediency of the course I was pursuing, so far as related to my scholars, I felt unmoved. Members of the church soon began to be alarmed, and rudely attacked

Brother Evans for suffering such innovations. The good man, you know, is one of the most prudent and cautious in the world; and began to query, whether I ought not, before introducing anything so novel, to have consulted the *Board of Trustees.* I presume *he* would have done so. Professor Farnsworth stood neutral. Esquire Quincy had witnessed our exercises, and highly approved; but he was absent on a journey. I felt rather anxious for the result of the matter, on the prosperity of the Seminary, and concluded to write to Mr. Simpson. He replied in these terms: 'I rejoice that you have taken a firm stand. If you relinquish it, yours be the blame.' Everything about that time seemed quiet, and I hoped that the scruples of Christians had been removed. I had invited every one who felt dissatisfied to come and see, and *then* judge. But to be brief, last Monday Deacon —— waited on me, and expressed great grief, on account of the feeling of the church generally; and represented the trial so serious, that he supposed many would decline communion on that account. He expressed for himself astonishment, that I should have been led to pursue such a course, but did not acknowledge any personal trial. If I had not at that time possessed uncommon presence of mind, I could not have supported such an onset. But I was not at all moved. I conversed with him very calmly, but could not remove his misapprehensions." She continued the calisthenic exercises, and finally, by demonstration, proved their utility.

CHAPTER VIII.

CHARACTER OF THE AFFECTIONS OF MISS H. — COMMENCEMENT OF CORRESPONDENCE WITH MR. JOSEPH SMITH, WITH A VIEW OF BECOMING ASSOCIATED WITH HIM AS A MISSIONARY.

NOTWITHSTANDING Miss H. acted independently, and in efficiency and strength exhibited masculine abilities, yet she was a woman in her affections. She loved tenderly, devotedly. This, however, was not her characteristic at an early period. We have seen that she was away from the tender influences of home from her seventh to her twelfth year. We have heard her say that the darling object of her heart, then, was to be first. We have seen her become subject to Christian influence, and to thirst to secure the approbation of Heaven. We have seen that two influences combined and nerved her to effort, till she arrived at what she esteemed the pinnacle of fame. Until this period she knew no desire but that of preferment. Her whole soul was absorbed in the thought of becoming useful, esteemed, and honored.

When she became a teacher, a new era commenced. Here was scope for the affections. A circle of young ladies, away from the influences of home, was thrown upon her care, claiming from her a mother's solicitude, a sister's love, and a Christian's affection. Now she awoke to a new existence. She lived for the public, thought of its approbation, and grasped, in her warm embrace, her pupils who leaned on her, as the source of everything desired. Many who read this will feel her fond arm around them, and the fervent pressure of affection's kiss. She loved all her pupils. They occupied her thoughts and her energies ; it was, however, as children. The love she received was reverential — it was ardent, almost to idolatry. Her pupils highly esteemed her, and wished to obey her precepts. She cherished and watched over them. But they were not friends to whom she might unbosom every thought, and receive advice and sympathy.

In the Principal of the Institution, Mr. Farnsworth, the Executive Board, and her Pastor, Mr. Evans, she felt that she had friends for counsel and trust. Her first associate, Miss Hadley, and her permanent associate after Miss H. left, were ever dear friends to her. These, and Misses Hall and Mitchell, members with her of Mr. E.'s family, and Misses L. A. Griggs and M. S. Patterson, her pupils, and for awhile teachers in the Seminary, constituted her social correspondents while at New Hampton.

At an early period of her teaching, her acquaintance commenced with Mr. Joseph Smith. He entered the institution at the time when she became

Principal of the female department. She met him at the social prayer meeting, esteemed his piety, and prized his active, energetic efforts to do good. After he became a member of the Theological Institution at Newton, she occasionally met him in Boston. An attachment was formed, and correspondence commenced. But months passed before there was a decided engagement. She felt that she was not her own, and that her chief inquiry should be, " Where can I labor, and how, with the best effect ? " Mr. Smith's future destination was uncertain, and she felt that she was not at liberty to act for herself until his course was to an extent determined.

Miss H.'s prepossessions were in favor of a missionary life. This she expressed publicly in the winter of 1832. In the conclusion of a communication for the Baptist Register, she says — " What is the reason that so few are devoting themselves to the missionary enterprise ? Is it because there are none who are ready to engage in the labor, or is it for want of money ? I think it cannot be the former, for if there are not hundreds in New England, who are ready and eager to engage as soon as a signal shall be given, and a way open, I am greatly mistaken. Is it, then, want of money ? Oh, let us blush ! Let us never call ourselves Christians, while we no more resemble our Lord. It was for our sakes he became poor, — and for what ? He has made us stewards; but, while his household are suffering for bread, we keep our purse closed, with the covetousness of Judas.

" Christian friends, what shall we do ? It cannot

be the duty of all to engage personally in the missionary labor. To those who thus pledge themselves will we solemnly pledge support and coöperation, and bid them God speed! But let not our benevolence stop here! Since, by the light of science, we are taught that the little sphere enclosed by mountains, in the midst of which we are placed, is not the limit of creation, let us extend our benevolence as wide as the range of our knowledge; and as we feel solicitous to procure for the members of our fireside circle every innocent gratification, and are careful to bestow every attention to render their enjoyment as complete as possible, let us seek the happiness of our fellow creatures, inspired not only by a noble glow of patriotism, inasmuch as we are citizens of the world, but feeling that we are members of the same family, with one common interest and one common Parent."

Miss H. did not allow herself to decide upon an engagement with Mr. Smith, except with entire reference to the claims of duty. In a letter to him, early in the spring of 1832, she says — " Ardent as my feelings are, I can suppress them, if duty requires; yes, however dear friendship may be, however sweet companionship of soul, however alluring the hopes of domestic life, I can, I will, resign all, whatever be the struggle, if duty calls. Upon that point I have been very anxious, and am still unsettled. Sometimes reason seems to say, quite audibly, If you will obey my dictates, the path is obvious. Then I resolve to act the heroine, to banish thoughts of love, and seek my happiness in contributing to the happiness of others. I conclude the exhaustless fountain of science, and the sweet consciousness of serving my generation, and my God, will render my life at least tolerable ; that by remaining unconnected, I shall subject myself to much less anguish, if I do not enjoy the most exquisite pleasures, of life ; that I may thus be able to form many minds to the love and practice of virtue, and thereby exert a very important influence over a large portion of the community. And is it not so ? Can I expect so large a sphere of action when differently circumstanced ? Possibly ! If so, I shall be happy. If not, I must submit. I feel that I am not at my own disposal. I have received everything from God, and to him everything is due. I wait the expression of His will ; and here I hardly dare express my sentiments, lest they should have some influence upon your determinations relative to your own duty. Here is the danger of a joint interest. Let me charge you to consult your own influence alone. Pursue independently your own course. Yours is a sacred office. Profane it not. My prayer shall be for your prosperity, and my ardent wish that you may excel in everything truly excellent.

" You ask me to pray for you. My dear sir, I never forget you when I remember myself at the mercy seat ; but I sometimes fear I have no interest there. If I could feel that consciousness of Divine approbation, which you experience, I should be very happy. Do pray that I may be satisfied of the will of God, be that what it may. If I can only be satisfied on that point, I shall be unmoved."

In another letter — " In respect to the subject con-

cerning which I expressed a want of satisfaction, my
mind is nearly at rest.   I believe I have discovered a
mistake under which I was laboring: I have been endeavoring to ascertain *now*, what the Lord will have
me do at a future time; whereas it seems to me now,
that I am to look to him for daily direction, no less
than for daily bread, and that if I am convinced of
my duty at the present time, I ought to be satisfied."

In the summer of 1832 several missionaries were
set apart at Boston.   Mr. Smith was present, and in
a letter to her, described the scene.   In reply, she
writes:

"I should have been very glad to witness the desig-
nation of the missionaries.   Great enterprises seem
glorious in the distance, but frequently excite other
emotions when nigh at hand.   I expect I have never
realized how great are the sacrifices attendant on the
missionary life.   There is but one thing about it
that strikes me with terror — that is, the possibility
of being left alone.   But if the Saviour was with me,
I should be supported even then.   I have thought
you might infer, from a casual remark, that should I
labor abroad, I should have a preference as to the
place.   This is not the fact.   The name of Burmah
is hallowed, and so great is the interest awakened for
that mission, that it will probably be well sustained.
If I had sufficient talent and enterprise, I should even
prefer some other station.

"But I only mention this, that you may see that I
am perfectly unbiased.   The child of Providence, I
would obey its dictates without reply.   I have sometimes thought, whether it were not love of fame, or

the influence of ambition, that prompted me to desire an uncommon path ; but I think I have felt, that if when I should leave the shore, my memory should be obliterated from the civilized world, and I should behold none observing to applaud my deeds, but Him who looks down from Heaven, I could be happy while endeavoring to lead the benighted to the Light of Life. I have been led to inquire too, if I might not faint under unexpected discouragements, and be brought at length to prefer a life of ease, to one of toil. I think, if my health should continue good, I could persevere. But I do not know what effect a sultry climate might have on my constitution. I sometimes feel almost invulnerable, but I know I am not so. I have felt recently, more than ever before, how entirely dependent I am upon my Heavenly Father for the inestimable blessing of health, and have been astonished that I have felt so little gratitude for a gift so constantly bestowed."

Had Mr. Smith become a missionary, as he at this time felt strongly inclined to be, it was his intention to throw himself, for support, principally upon the churches in New Hampshire, his native state, in the hope, by this arrangement, of awakening among them a deeper interest in the missionary cause. The better to prepare the way for the accomplishment of this purpose, when her destiny might, as she now began to anticipate, become permanently united with his, Miss H. decided to remain at New Hampton.

This season, Misses E. and S. were added to the board of teachers.

8

CHAPTER IX.

THE spring of 1832, Miss Hazeltine had an opportunity to become a teacher at the West. The circumstances are developed in the following letter to Miss P. P. Rand, dated Boston, March 27, 1832.

" Nothing has occurred here of much interest to us since you left, except that Mr. Going has been laboring in this city for the West. He lectured on Sabbath afternoon at Dr. Sharp's, on the situation and the wants of that section of country. His statements were very candid, and to me, intensely interesting. He has just called and spent an hour with me, in conversation on the subject of our emigration to Granville. He manifested the same candor here, which always characterizes him ; but seems to coincide entirely with the views expressed by Mr. Pratt in the communication to J. W. Rand, which I shall transcribe.

'At a meeting of the trustees of the Granville Female Seminary, held last evening, you were unanimously invited to become principal of the seminary, and Miss Martha Hazeltine first female teacher, and

Miss Philinda P. Rand assistant. · It was voted that you be requested to repair to this place as soon as practicable, and commence operations. Also, that you should adjust the terms, regulations, &c., as your judgment may dictate, after you arrive, and receive the avails of the school as your compensation, making the division among yourselves, according to your mutual agreement.'

"It seems really very important that we should go on immediately. But I think we cannot, possibly, before August. Do you think we can? On the other hand must we stay at New Hampton through both terms? or must we not go at all?"

At this period the character of the scholars, and the high reputation of the school demanded great skill and forethought in management. Miss H. appreciated this truth, and with her usual adroitness in adapting herself to exigences, resolved to secure teachers qualified for different departments, and thus, by a division of labor, attain a degree of efficiency and excellence, that would otherwise have been impossible. Miss R. retained the department of drawing. Miss E. was elected to fill the department of the natural sciences, Miss S. that of mathematics, and Miss H. retained for herself the department of languages. This was the first step in establishing the elevated rank of the school upon a permanent base. This summer term, in a letter dated July, she thus writes to Miss Hadley: — "I do not know but you have lost your interest in New Hampton scenes, and so I will not be very prolix. I believe we have sixty-five scholars, very studious, and well disposed. I have Miss Everett and Miss Sleeper besides Miss Rand. Everything moves on very easily, never more so."

Miss H. soon after this period was destined to have her connection at New Hampton almost entirely changed. She had been resident there four seasons, and the school had been constantly advancing. For two years she had boarded in the family of the Rev. Mr. Evans, and had become attached to all its members. It had become her home. She had learned also to enter into all the plans of Professor Farnsworth, for promoting the advancement of the institution, and had come to feel, that its prosperity was identified with his presence and efforts; and in Miss Rand she had found a firm, trustworthy friend. These seemed the chief ties, which bound her to New Hampton. But in the winter of 1833, all, in an important sense, were severed.

Professor F. resigned as principal of the institution, for a location at the South. Miss H. writes at this time to a friend: "All before me is uncertain. In relation to New Hampton, we live by the day. Professor F. leaves in the spring. I have no assurance I shall be here another season. I feel that I must watch the interests of the seminary. Perhaps it is not destined to be sustained long. The providences of God look doubtful, but I hope I shall not move without a divine signal."

Miss Rand was taken ill, left the seminary, and before the opening of the spring term, was numbered with the dead. Soon after her death, Miss

H. visited her mother, and thus describes the circumstances to Mr. Smith. "I arrived at Bedford about four o'clock, P. M., and upon opening the door, was nearly certain of the awful sequel. For a moment I felt as if I could not possibly stay, and stepping back requested the driver not to be in haste. Then advancing into the house, I met an aged woman, whom I knew, from her resemblance to Philinda, to be her mother. I asked her how she did? She replied by asking me if I was Miss Hazeltine. Then pressing my hand in her own, burst into an agony of tears. By this time I had come to myself enough, to request the driver to call for me on Monday, and sitting down by the fire, learned, from Miss Rand's mother, that she had died a week before, and was buried on Monday. I can never describe my feelings, as I was sitting in that solitary house, with none but the lonely, bereaved mother, nor the emotion of joy I felt, when a sister, strongly resembling Philinda, entered the door. It had seemed to me that all things were coming to an end, that nought but desolation was spread around. As this sister entered, I felt a thrill of comfort, as if somebody yet lived. After a little while another sister entered, and soon after her father. He is a venerable, godly man, intimately acquainted with the Scriptures, and bringing strongly to my mind, the image of Apostolic times. I felt as if on holy ground, surrounded by a holy atmosphere, and almost feared to profane the sacred place. Her friends had reserved her papers undisturbed for me. As soon as I began to read them the horror of the scene passed away, I felt as if I could converse calmly with the dead. Her journal was very complete. She made allusions to many incidents which I recollected perfectly well, and her style of writing and her penmanship were so familiar, that I seemed to enjoy her society. Her grave was but a few steps off, within the view of her parents, and as if beneath their care, and I felt that she rested in peace. She was sick but little more than a fortnight, with dropsy in the head — had her reason only at short intervals, during which she was always engaged in singing or prayer, or in expressions of affection to her friends. She called my name, frequently, with great earnestness, but I think it was all for the best I was not there. Her wildness and distress would have made a very melancholy impression upon my mind. Miss Woodman was with her during her illness, and tarried with her friends till after her burial. I feel that she is happy. She peacefully sleeps in the silent grave, free from trouble, pain and warfare. She had previously endured the most severe conflicts, in her mind, but came out of the furnace like gold. We shall never see her again below, but she speaks loudly from the papers she has left. I think I never felt so deeply abased as when I read her diary. ' Blessed are the dead that die in the Lord.'

> I entered, but no well-known voice was heard,
> No footstep lightly tripped to meet me ; — all
> Was silent as the tomb.   And is she gone,
> My loved Philinda !   Shall I greet her smile
> No more, and ne'er again exchange the kiss
> Affectionate ?   She lies in yonder grave !
> The whit'ning marble rises to my view,
> Beyond the lovely church.

And is it thou,
My loved associate, companion, friend,
The partner of my joys! And shall I ne'er
With thee hold sweet communion?
 Ah, this her mother dear! with hands pressed close
To mine, and streaming eyes. ' She 's gone, she 's gone!
Long we 've waited thee, and oft, full oft
She called thy name in tones of sweet affection.
O to my mind thou bringest her very form,
As if herself were here. Weep, weep with us,
For God has laid his hand a second time
With awful weight upon us, and chastised
Us, very sore.'
   Yes, thou afflicted mother,
Father beloved, brothers and sisters dear,
I weep with you. Yea, weep ye too with me,
Now left to brave the storms of life, bereft
Of this support. O how shall I alone
Sustain the burden which we both have borne?
 But why repine? She would not thus advise.
Have we no God in whom to trust, on whom
Rely? Have we forgot his gracious word,
His cheering promise? Do we not well know
That whom he loves, wisely he oft chastises? —
Then let us meekly bow beneath the rod,
For 't is to heal, he wounds us, and to bless,
That he afflicts.
   Nor does she cease to speak
Though dead. E'n from the grave we hear her voice
In strains of deepest piety, and love
Sincere, exhorting to a life unspotted,
To holy thoughts, and deeds of pure benevolence.
Shall we not strive to emulate her virtues,
And to attain that meetness for the bliss
Of heaven which she possessed? —
And long the grave cannot retain her, sown
A mortal body, she will rise immortal,
O glorious hope! we rise e'en now in thought,
A holy throng, to meet our Lord, to be
Forever with him. Let us then refrain
From weeping, and rejoice, as Jesus bids
Us evermore.

Mr. Evans removed his family to Canaan. Miss H. says, in a letter at this time, " I feel like a bird thrown from its nest. Whether I can spread my wings, and sustain myself in the broad expanse, remains to be proved."

She writes to Miss Mitchell, a member of Mr. Evans's family : " You are still at your quiet home. I do not allow myself to envy you, though I think you highly favored. Endeavor to improve your rich opportunities to grow in grace. I did not value my privileges, sufficiently, when I lived in your pleasant family. It was like a father's house to me, and the remembrance is hallowed. In my mind it will ever be associated with pleasant thoughts. I cannot find, anywhere in all the wanderings of imagination, any spot which conveys to my mind, so lively an image of rest, as your peaceful abode."

During this season of doubt and uncertainty, she was still perplexed with regard to her connection with Mr. Smith. She thus writes to him in a letter in the winter of 1833, Dec. 6. " I have been inclined to distrust the faithfulness of God in respect to his care of his creatures. I am reading Old Testament history, particularly with the design of studying sacred geography ; and have noticed the frequent instances in which the Old Testament saints asked counsel of God, and received direct responses ; and have thought, O ! that I might be thus privileged ; but alas ! he does not now regard ; he will not deign to answer. 'Tis true I am not worthy that the King of kings should condescend to guide me, but whom then have I for a guide ? I know that I am exceedingly sinful, an unworthy offering; but such as I am, I have given myself to the Lord, and is it not all that I can do? Will he not graciously lead me? Will he not in some way manifest his pleasure? What can I do without his direction? O Lord God, deny me not an expression of thy will. I have this day solemnly renewed my vow, if the Lord will make me feel satisfied in relation to my future duty, by his assistance, as long as I live, I will be entirely his. I am resolved still to confide in God, and trust that in his own due time he will make me be at peace. It seems to me that I feel prepared for the worst. God has balm for the bleeding heart, and can heal the wounded spirit. Whatever he does is right, and though I faint he can sustain me. O will he not signify to me his pleasure, that I may do his will?

"You speak of grief, that you are a cause of anxiety to me; on the other hand, it is a source of great grief to me that I perplex you so much by my indecision. I could here say much, did I not hope to see you soon. Suffice it to say, I should feel perfectly quiet, were I not afraid of disappointing you. May the Lord preserve me from ever rendering you unhappy.

"Respecting the missionaries, I am anticipating a rich repast in conversing with you. You have indeed enjoyed a peculiar privilege, of which you will make me in no small degree a partaker. You have an opportunity of calculating coolly, and of counting the cost of a missionary life. It requires, I think, great moral courage. I have been praying that if it is my duty to engage in an enterprise so sublime, the Lord would give me 'another heart,' to use an expression made in relation to Saul, about the time he was anointed king over Israel.   Perhaps the allusion is obscure.   I have endeavored to bring the subject nearer, and to make it seem real.   I have some of the recoilings of nature, and some fearful shrinkings from an apprehension lest I might engage in the work unbidden.   I feel peaceful for the present, although not such a conviction as to encourage me to hope I shall not hereafter be similarly affected. You speak of selfishness in your prayers.   I have feared that the burden of my prayer has been, that I might feel that I am in the path of duty.   But I have tried to leave it wholly with the Lord, regardless of consequences.   He will do 'all things well.'

"I asked my father, the other day, why he was not willing I should become a missionary; 'because,' said he, 'I believe you will wish, when it is all in vain, that you had been contented in your native land.   Besides, I think,' said he, 'that the most conscientious may mistake in respect to their duty.   I hope Mr. Smith will think differently from what he does now by the time he is prepared to *settle*.'

"All this question lies with God, and it is he alone who must determine it.   If I should feel fully satisfied of my duty, I think I should not want courage. But, in this respect, I have suffered much, and my faith has been severely tried.   I cannot yet help feeling, at times, to urge my request for special direction relative to the most important events of future life, with an importunity which can take no denial.   The question seems so momentous in its consequences, that I feel utterly unable to decide it.

"I have been exceedingly troubled, when I have contemplated the instances, which have occurred within the circle of my knowledge, of pious ladies, who have sought the Lord much for direction in this respect, and yet have found themselves very unhappily connected. When reflecting upon these facts, a query arises, 'Does God regard such matters, and is it of any avail to pray to him?' If I answer these questions in the negative, and form the solemn marriage contract on my own responsibility, the foundation of all religious action, in future life, is destroyed, for the only principles which could inspire me with courage are annihilated.

"Miss S. had a letter from Miss —— the other day. She seems sad. What a fund of intelligence and goodness she possesses.

> 'Full many a gem of purest ray serene,
> The dark, unfathomed caves of ocean bear,
> Full many a flower is born to blush unseen,
> And waste its sweetness on the desert air.'

"I could weep at this sentiment. She is more worthy of you than I am."

CHAPTER X.

At the opening of the fifth season of school, we find Miss H. at her accustomed station at New Hampton. She felt that, probably, she should not teach many years; and should she go out as a missionary, it was her wish to occupy some new station, and place herself under the patronage of the Baptists in New Hampshire. With this plan in view, she still continues to teach in the Seminary, feeling that it would be for her ultimate interest, and the general good, to continue identified with her native state, and particularly with the school at New Hampton, then the principal institution of the New Hampshire Baptists. The success of the school is, from this time, undoubted.

June, 1833, she thus writes to Mrs. Hadley —
" We have entered ninety-seven pupils, so that, with the teachers, you see, we have a hundred. This is pretty well, for us — quite enough. We do not want an unwieldy, complicated thing, you know.

" We have a fine speaker. I am much pleased with

him. I suppose you know it is Professor Smith. I am almost as well acquainted with him already, as with those who have been here a long time. He has no haughty ways, is one of the kindest persons you ever saw, and yet unyieldingly firm. Miss Nutting is the teacher in drawing. Miss S. and myself board with Mrs. Nash. I have taken the responsibility of appointing L. A. Griggs teacher of English literature. She is doing admirably."

At this time she gave a decided answer to Mr. Smith. The letter announcing her decision, was dated May, 1833. The following is an extract :

" In what attitude shall I imagine you this evening — oppressed with anxiety about yourself, but, above all, grieved with your best friend ? I have given you pain — I have troubled you, and why ? I can only say I knew not what to do. I have felt so much, and reasoned so much, and pleaded so much, to know my duty, to no effect, that I felt, at last, I could no longer sustain the struggle. I was aware that, to avoid the unhappiness of indecision, I should be prone to take refuge in the hopes and prospects I had fondly cherished, whether consistent with duty or not ; and, to counteract this propensity, I thought to banish the subject entirely from my mind. I felt that I was abusing your affection, and consequently that I was unworthy of it ; and I finally felt so much subdued as to care little for myself, and thought, if you could make another happy, consistently with your own feelings, I ought to be willing. Be assured I never cherished one thought that you were incon-

9

stant or divided in your affections — O, no! I have ever regarded them as my own most entirely.

"This *hand* — this *heart* — *myself,* shall be yours. Your sorrows, your joys, shall henceforth be mine. Do not give yourself one anxious thought — I am yours, and prefer to share your lot. May heaven forbid that this heart should ever waver, these feelings ever change.

"In relation to your future destination, I have thought seriously. I have feared I might have been indirectly the means of diverting you from that course which would have led you to the field of labor, on which your heart was fixed, and for which God designed you. Should you be prevented by my means from acting with the greatest effect in the cause of the Redeemer, how perfectly wretched it would make me. You have told me you did feel satisfied of your duty in relation to your collegiate course. If you are not honestly convinced on this point, I beseech you not to yield to my wishes; rather change your whole course, independently of me.

"You may wish to know why I feel so much satisfaction, and may be led to fear it arises from the influence of sympathetic affection. I think not. I think I feel that kind of evidence, which has given me so much satisfaction in times past, in relation to particular questions. There is no longer a conflict of arguments; so far as it regards myself, obstacles vanish, and every consideration seems to corroborate my decision. Now, should my Heavenly Father send misfortunes and afflictions, I can buffet the billows, and act the Christian heroine. So may God enable me to do."

In her next letter, she says — "I have generally felt peaceful since I wrote you, although I have sometimes feared that I wrote with too much assurance and enthusiasm. But you know what I mean. I did not intend to wrest the matter from the hands of God, or to signify that I had any miraculous communications upon the subject; but only that I felt satisfied, and abhorred such indecision as I had manifested. I hope we shall still feel that we are to be guided by Providence, and hold ourselves in readiness to yield to the will of our Heavenly Father."

Miss Hazeltine's engagement with Mr. Smith was no act of a moment; it was under contemplation for months, and this letter, announcing her decision, shows that she had felt deeply, suffered intensely, and long made the issue a subject of prayer. Her friends love to contemplate her at this period. She was Principal of a Ladies' Seminary and had ample scope for the exercise of a vigorous intellect — was teacher of biblical literature and moral science, and could gratify her desire to communicate her own exalted views of God, the gospel, and the dignity of the divine economy; and in her associates, in carrying forward her pupils in an elevated course of education, and her special friend, she found objects upon which to bestow her overflowing affections. The history of this period is, in one sense, the history of her life. This was the noontime of her day of usefulness and happiness. Her sun now shone in his strength and brightness. It might have been well said of her, 'she now lives.'

CHAPTER XI.

PERHAPS no act in the life of Miss H. showed more grasp of thought, or tended more to secure a lasting and extensive influence, than the formation of the Literary and Missionary Association in the Seminary at New Hampton. It was then a new project; indeed, it may be said to have originated entirely with herself. Few can realize the greatness of the act but those who witness the results; few can realize the impulse it gives to mind, or its value as a means of benevolence. Speaking, in the first annual report, of the general prosperity of the Seminary, Miss H. says, "The most interesting feature of improvement, of which we can make mention, is to be found in the advantages afforded us by our Literary and Missionary Association. Although my expectations of the results of this Society were, from the first, so sanguine as to seem, even to myself, to partake of the romantic, I can truly say, that they have hitherto been more than realized. Talents are by this means brought to light and cultivated, which might otherwise have remained forever concealed. I have often been delightfully surprised at discovering the beautiful ' gems of the mountains,' thus unknowingly brought together." The Society was, indeed, designed to call into action literary talent, stimulate to the acquisition of knowledge, and to become a bond of union among the members of the school. Now pupils came for a term, then returned to their friends and were forgotten. Those that left loved their alma mater, but there were no means of becoming acquainted with its interests. They would with ready hand have contributed to its elevation, and coöperated in all its designs. Here was a means by which it could be accomplished. An association could be organized, officers elected, and a means of communication instituted between all that should become members of the Seminary.

But it was necessary that this Society should have some end in view which should equally interest all. This was found in the missionary enterprise, which at once enlisted the sympathies of all, and would continue to be a subject of interest until the kingdoms of the world should become the kingdom of God. Miss H. first presented the subject in the summer of 1833. She writes in a letter at this time —

" We are making an attempt to form an association among the young ladies of the Seminary for the promotion of foreign missions, nominally. My real object is not less the general benefit which I hope will accrue to every benevolent institution by means of such an association. We intend to have membership continued after the young ladies leave the Seminary, and to enlist as many as we can during

each successive term. Thus you see in a few years
we · shall become quite numerous, and shall have
it in our power to do almost anything, if it be true
that 'women govern the world.' We intend to issue
an annual report, addressed to each member of the
association, containing items gathered from correspondence, and such matter as may be interesting,
and if we get a constitution which pleases us, we
mean to have Mrs. Wade's name at least on our list.
We shall make provision for honorary members, and
thus obtain several ladies of distinction to coöperate
with us."

In the fall she writes to Mr. S.

" We are prosperous and happy at present. Have
succeeded in forming our Literary and Missionary
Society. Elected Mrs. Wade, Mrs. Mason, Misses
H. Griggs, E. Maynard, and J. B. Leaveritt, honorary members. They have done me the honor to ap-
point me Corresponding Secretary, and I have just
been writing a letter in my official capacity to Mrs.
Mason.

" The constitution adopted requires each individual
to pay fifty cents annually, while connected with the
Seminary, and twenty-five cents annually afterward.
The funds thus received, after the payment of the
expense of the association, are to be appropriated in
aid of missions by the board of officers.

" It was made the duty of each member to communicate to the corresponding secretary, annually, facts,
in a literary article, with the design of promoting the
interests of literature and missions. And the secretary was required to publish, in the annual report, an

abstract of all communications, and such original matter as she might herself contribute, and to forward a copy of the same to each member of the association."

May 9, 1834, a code of by-laws was adopted which required the association to meet on the Wednesday succeeding the first Monday of each month, as a missionary society; and every Wednesday excepting the one following the first Monday, as a literary society. The parts to be performed at each meeting were to be assigned by a committee of three.

There was at this time connected with the Seminary, a class designing to become teachers of high schools. These were justly distinguished for energy, piety, and principle. They gave character to the Society, tone to its spirit, and elevation to its performances. The first soliciting committee, a committee chosen from the active members of the society, were, Susan M. Griggs, now the wife of Rev. E. L. Magoon; Eveline Belnap, wife of Rev. C. Parker; Hadassah Stevens, at present teacher of a celebrated school at Madison, Ill.; Caroline Nevens, afterwards the wife of the Rev. E. Crane; Mary P. Merriam, the wife of T. B. White, professor in the college at Wake Forest, N. C.; and Adelaide Haines, at present wife of the Rev. D. P. Cilley. Of the first committee of assignments, Miss Mary Ann Brown, now the wife of Rev. William Leverett, professor of the college at Upper Alton, Ill.; Mila S. Carpenter, wife of the Rev. Mr. Currier, missionary at Milgrove, Ind.; and Aurilia A. Barker, wife of the Rev.

Mr. Burbank, principal of the Buck Creek Seminary, Shelbyville, Ky.

Miss Hazeltine acted as corresponding secretary as long as she was connected with the seminary, and during this period published five annual reports. The following is from the first, printed at Concord in the spring of 1835.

To the Members of the Association.

"DEAR LADIES, — Although in performing the duties before me, I am to act as your corresponding secretary, I find it impossible to divest myself of those tender associations arising from the relation which you formerly sustained to me, and beg you will pardon me, if I dispense with the formalities which might otherwise be expected, and address you rather as an individual.

The privilege which I now enjoy, is one to which I have long looked forward with ardent desire. Even before this association was formed, or the plan of its operations divulged, the anticipation, visionary as it might seem, of being able to address, at once, so many of my dear pupils, often filled my mind with a kind of ecstatic delight. Through the indulgence of Heaven, I am permitted this day to realize these darling hopes.

It would afford me the highest gratification once more to behold you all, and to listen to your varied narratives. Often as I have cast my eye over the catalogue of your names, imagination has painted you present before me, with so much of reality, that I could hardly forbear exclaiming with Æneas, 'cur dextræ jungere dextram non datur, ac veras audire et reddere voces.' But though the time is no more, with regard to many of us, in which we may enjoy personal intercourse, it should be to us a source of unfeigned gratitude, that we are not, on this account, under the necessity of consigning, to oblivion, friendships sincere and ardent as I trust ours are, but that, in the silent language of the pen, we may still hold sweet communion.

In taking a brief view of the present situation of those who once mingled with us in the most endearing intercourse, we find that many of them are already occupying places of high responsibility. How great the amount of this influence may be, it is impossible to calculate. Whether this influence will be beneficial, and that in a high degree, will depend very much upon the education they have received. Such reflections as these have come home, with great solemnity, to my mind, and have caused me to inquire, whether I have contributed all in my power to qualify them to discharge well the duties of their present stations. That I have not been guilty of deliberate remissness or negligence, I feel conscious. That I have often and greatly failed through incompetency, I doubt not. If I could, I would gladly make amends for such deficiency ; but though I cannot hope to retrieve the errors of the past, I may, through the report, offer suggestions, which may be of some practical advantage."

At an early period after the Society was formed, the foundation for a library was laid. The year after

Miss Hazeltine writes in a communication to the acting members:

"Those who came forward so magnanimously, something less than a year since, for the establishment of a library, will be pleased to learn that our catalogue of books now numbers eighty volumes, and that we have thirty-six dollars and fifty cents in the treasury to be appropriated to this object.

In relation to the interests of the Society, we are happy to say that God has blessed us the past year with a degree of prosperity hitherto unexampled, both with respect to numbers and degree of attainment. The dews of divine grace have also distilled upon us with peculiar sweetness, so that we feel ourselves specially called upon to bless the name of the Lord.

We feel confident that you will continue to cherish an affectionate interest in our prosperity, and pledge ourselves to remember you, especially at each return of our missionary meeting: and we pray that you may all be as missionaries, sent forth to bless the world in the various stations to which providence may have called you; and may the God of all grace constantly enrich your hearts with the choicest influences of his Holy Spirit.

To the Honorary Members.

Dear Ladies, — In taking the liberty of electing you honorary members of the association, we acted from the assurance that you were friends to literature and to missions, and in the confidence that you would not scorn to lend your aid to the humblest efforts, if sincere and well-directed, for the promotion of these objects. Pardon us then, if in aught we have been too sanguine; we prefer no claim to your coöperation, but simply present before you the nature and plan of our operations, for your countenance or disapprobation. It is to you, nevertheless, that our young ladies must chiefly look, for lessons of practical life; those lessons, of all others, the most important. From want of actual experience, their teachers cannot be qualified, in the highest sense, for this department of education. In your several spheres of action, you are brought into contact with almost every variety of human condition; you know the evils existing in society, you know their causes, and you know the remedy. Could you enter our hall at a meeting of our Society, and behold it closely lined with young ladies, more than half of whom are members of Christian churches, in a course of preparation for the same duties you are daily required to perform, actually assembled for the express purpose of receiving instruction to this very end, I am persuaded you could not find it in your hearts to withhold from them such lessons as your own experience would enable you to impart. How varied and how rich the mass of instruction that would be poured into our associations might we be favored with only one communication from each of you in a season. How cheering, when met to do what we can for our own improvement, to feel that kind friends abroad are interested for us, and are reaching forth a maternal hand, to help us up the ruggid acclivity of life. Series of letters upon the various topics connected with the sphere of woman, would do us incalculable good; but if this is too much to ask, may we not expect, at least, an expression of your sympathetic regard?

To those who have kindly favored us with their correspondence the past season, permit us to tender our heartfelt thanks. Your letters have contributed materially to our prosperity, not only by their direct influence upon the young ladies, but by the support and encouragement they have afforded the immediate officers. Let me then, in my own behalf, and in behalf of my associates in duty, respectfully present you our warmest acknowledgments. While we desire to have the honor of being co-workers with yourselves in that which is good, we would hope not to forfeit the unequivocal tokens of your kind approbation.

Yours, with affectionate respect,

M. HAZELTINE, *Cor. Sec.*"

Subsequently, she writes to the same: "Might I be permitted, without incurring the charge of self-interest, I would plead in behalf of our Seminary? We have hitherto labored under circumstances of untold disadvantage. Plans are now laid and in part effected, by which our exertions may be rendered vastly more productive, and we hope tell more effectually upon the intelligent and future usefulness of our pupils. Our library shelves are not filled. Will you not send us respectively some new and approved work, as it issues from the press? Have you no volumes of the British classics or poets which would be invested at better interest where they will be kept constantly in circulation, than where they now are?

Will not some society, in the spirit of Dover and Nashua, send us the Family or Christian Library? the Encyclopedia of Religious Knowledge? Webster's large English Dictionary? Have you not some rare specimens of geology, mineralogy, or conchology, for our cabinet, or dried flowers for an herbarium? These things, insignificant as they may seem in themselves, will leave their impress, modified and combined in a thousand ways, upon the imperishable tablet of a thousand minds.

" As a missionary society, our prospects were never more encouraging. The Lord of the harvest has, as we trust, one from our number, whom he will account worthy to bear his name to the distant heathen. Another is expecting ere long to embark, and we are confident there are still others who are only waiting for the voice, ' Whom shall we send, and who for us will go?' to reply with throbbing heart, ' Send me.' Often has our spirit died within us while we have witnessed those whose emotions have been so deep, so self-devoted, so irrepressible, so much, in fine, resembling what we conceive to be felt by those solemnly called by God to the sacred ministry, pining because they might not tell the perishing heathen that Christ died for sinners. Those only, to the sanctuary of whose souls such disclosures have been made, and whose response has been awaited as the oracle of God, can tell the anguish of the moment, when compelled to reply in language for which our souls misgave us, or turn silently away. God grant such may never again be our painful experience.

" The promptness of your letters upon the subject

10

of raising a fund, by voluntary contribution, for the
purpose of education,* affords us the most gratifying

* The following is the history of the *education department* of
the Literary and Missionary Association.

Oct. 27, 1836. A special meeting was called by order of the
President.

The Society having assembled, the President remarked, that
hitherto our efforts in behalf of missions had been necessarily
somewhat restricted ; that an opportunity now offered of acting
more directly and efficiently in this cause ; and that the object of
the present meeting was to take the subject into consideration,
and adopt such measures as should be judged expedient.

By leave of the President, the corresponding secretary, Miss
Hazeltine, observed, that something more than a year before, a
young lady, J. B. Leavitt, a member of the Association, had conversed with her in relation to devoting herself personally to the
work of missions — that she was, at that time, deeply affected
with her case, and desirous of devising some means of enabling
her to obtain the preparation requisite for the sphere she so
ardently longed to occupy ; but, reflecting upon the infancy and
limited resources of the Association, she saw no possible way of
affording her any immediate and efficient aid ; that the same
young lady had at length formed the resolution to make known
her convictions to the church of which she was a member — that
she had done so, and had received a full and warm expression of
their approbation and sympathy — that the Pastor of this church
had communicated these facts to herself, adding that the church
were not well able to afford her the assistance she needed, and
that he hoped the Association would regard it their privilege to
assume this responsibility ; — that for herself she believed they
were *now able* to do so ; and that she felt strongly impressed with
the conviction that the decision of the present question involved
solemn responsibilities.

Misses Rogers, Johnson and some others, having spoken of
their acquaintance with the lady referred to, and of their belief
that the measure proposed was both expedient and practicable,
on motion of Miss Harriet A. Willard, seconded by Miss Sarah
Newton,

Resolved, that the Association make an effort to educate the
lady proposed ; and that a committee be elected, as assistants to
the corresponding secretary, to communicate with the absent

assurance that your aid will never be withheld when required in a similar cause.   We have not yet, it is

acting and honorary members on this subject, soliciting their counsel and coöperation.

Many of the Honorary Members wrote, strongly recommending the measures proposed.

Jan. 3, 1837 — Appointed as a committee to consider the desirableness and practicability of extending the operations of the society in the cause of female education, Misses Mary A. Spaulding, Judith Leavitt, Jane Cummings, and Ruth O. Dow.   They reported as follows : —

We feel that the subject submitted for our investigation, demands the serious attention of this society, as friends of literature and missions.   It is highly important that Christians, as individuals, and as associate bodies, should accurately appreciate their ability, and carefully select those channels of operation in which this ability may be exerted to the best advantage.   That we have it in our power, as a body, to effect more than we are now doing in the cause of benevolence, can scarce be doubted ; and that the object which has been proposed, as inviting our charities, is a laudable one, seems to us equally obvious.   If a female is to become a missionary in the East, she needs extensive knowledge ; if a missionary in the West, she needs it ; if a teacher in her own land or indeed a Christian mother, she surely requires it.   That there are many females of eminent piety destitute of the means of education, and consequently destined to exert but a limited influence in the Christian world, who, with but little assistance, might become extensively useful, is an unquestionable truth. With these views of the subject, we beg leave to submit the following suggestions : —

That Female Education be henceforth considered as a distinct object of our Association ; and that, as this object is not specifically recognised in our present name, we be henceforth known in our associated capacity as The Young Ladies' Literary and Missionary Association and Education Society of the New Hampton Female Seminary. .

We would also recommend, that a Prudential Board be elected, from such of our honorary members as can be present at our annual meetings, to coöperate with the Executive in presiding over this department of our operations.

Should this plan meet the approbation of those present, we

true, received pledges for the proposed object, to the amount that will be necessary ; but we have not a

would suggest the propriety of submitting the subject to our absent acting and honorary members, and that they be requested to be present at the next annual meeting, or to send by letter, previous to that time, an expression of their feelings on this question.

Voted that this report be accepted.

This subject was thus presented at the subsequent annual meeting, Aug. 15, 1838.

Having elected the board of officers and honorary members, the subject of annexing female education, as a distinct branch, to the objects hitherto embraced by the society, was presented for consideration.

Mrs. Professor Brown then remarked, that the object now claiming the attention of the society, had long lain near her heart ; that it presented a sphere of benevolence loudly demanding our efforts; that the measures proposed met with her entire concurrence, and, if adopted, should receive her hearty coöperation.

Miss Elizabeth E. Farnsworth, of Newport, observed, that nothing could more deeply enlist her sympathies than the plan now before the association ; that she had long deplored the condition of those in whom the fire of genius had been quenched, and the ardent desire for usefulness repressed by the hard hand of penury ; that she felt that the object of the society was a most praiseworthy one, and that there was abundant power successfully to carry forward the enterprise, could it be brought to bear upon the point in question.

Mrs. Rev. Benjamin Brierly, of Somersworth, and Miss Ruth S. Robinson, Principal of the Seminary, Townsend, Mass., and several other acting members then present from a distance, expressed their entire approbation of the measures proposed ; and, upon motion, it was unanimously

Voted, That female education be henceforth considered as a distinct object of the association, and that the constitution be so amended, as distinctly to recognise and fully to provide for it.

The necessity of securing more ample funds for the current expenses of the society was then presented, and a subscription opened for this object.

The following was from the Circular of Miss Hazeltine this year :

doubt the funds will be forthcoming when needed. May God graciously accept the offering at your hand.

" Dear Ladies,— Allow me, in this place, to invite your attention to the present attitude of the association, in reference to benevolent effort. By a careful perusal of the last and the present report, you will have already ascertained what has been done, and where a helping hand is at this moment needed. As a literary society, we have nothing to ask, except for our cabinet and library. The missionary department is now very much identified with that of education. The last-named object, as a branch of benevolent effort, claims, at the present time, our especial attention. The desirableness of such an institution, as a charitable education society for the benefit of females, has, for the two past years, been amply discussed, not only in the association, as composed of youthful individuals, but by our honorary members, in the wisdom of whose decision we have the fullest cause to confide. We find, at present, but one voice upon the subject. We have, therefore, taken incipient measures — have actually prosecuted the education of one young lady to a point which might warrant her entering upon the duties, either of a missionary to the heathen, or of principal of a literary seminary in a civilized land ; another is pursuing her studies, mostly sustained by private benefactions ; and a third is hoping soon to resume, under the auspices of the society, the studies so indispensable to distinguished usefulness, but which necessity had compelled her to abandon. We want, now, that all the ladies of our churches should come up to this work, each according to her ability. The number who are in pressing want of aid, we should not dare to estimate, if we were able, lest the view might altogether discourage. But we can sustain the three already upon our list, and, with the coöperation of our sisters, many others. We ask pious ladies, wives of ministers and deacons, and other influential individuals, if there is not some one in your church, who, you heartily wish, could enjoy the advantages of education ? Are you not troubled for such an one ? Does not conscience often whisper in your ear, that you are losing time, that you are wasting talent, by withholding your exertions in her behalf ? If your hearts respond in the affirmative to these questions, let me ask you if you have looked around you, to see what resources may be brought to bear upon the point — how much may be obtained from the immediate friends and acquaintances of the young lady, towards

10*

" Sisters pray for us, that the present season may be
one of special reviving.   Visit us always when you
can, and need I repeat it, we shall look for, and expect at least one letter from each of you during the
season.   Please inform us of the state of literature

procuring for her the desired advantages?   Having done this, let
the result be known, and peradventure some sister church will
help you.   The experiment, at least, can be made.

Two societies have been formed upon the principle here exhibited.   Of these, the one at Meredith is laboring for our first beneficiary, who is a member of the church in that place.   That at
Peterborough has, as yet, no candidate, but stands ready to help
some society which may not be able quite to support its own.
We think societies of this kind might be formed in almost every
church, certainly every country church, where the calls for charitable effort are comparatively few.   We believe they would do
some churches good, that they would effect more than almost any
one means besides, to promote their spirituality and the growth
of religion in the hearts of their members.

We ask, then, that as soon as may be, in the coming season,
such societies may be formed, and, if agreeable, report themselves
our auxiliaries, that they may avail themselves of the advantages
of the association, according to the provisions of our constitution,
as amended.

Dear Sisters, accept our annual salutations.   May the God of
all grace dwell with you richly the present year, and may our
next report present the most cheering accounts of your abound-
ing in consolation, and in fruit, to the glory of God.

Yours very affectionately,
M. Hazeltine, Cor. Sec'y."

Since the period to which reference is made above, Miss Leavitt, the first beneficiary, has married the Rev. Mr. Jones, and
sailed as missionary to Siam.   Experience proves that the adoption of education, as a branch of benevolent effort, was made in
wisdom.   Every year has witnessed some addition to the means
for aiding this department of influence.   The past year, August,
1841, it was voted that any lady, though she might never have
been a member of the school, might become a life member of the
society by paying $5 at a time.   It is now believed that this

and the spirit of missions in your particular societies or neighborhoods, and accept the Annual Report in return. You will have our warmest wishes, and we shall remember you especially at every missionary meeting with Christian affection."

branch of the society's operations will become extensively useful. There have been, the past year, two beneficiaries.

Three years since a consociating association was formed at Philadelphia. This society has ever been highly approved by its members, and is at present considered by the officers of the school with which it is connected as one of the greatest auxiliaries in the progress of an education.

CHAPTER XII.

DURING the summer of 1833, there was an extensive revival. The circumstances are developed in the following letter to Mr. S.: —

"Through the great kindness of God, I am permitted to write you good tidings to-night. We hope the Lord is here by the influences of his Holy Spirit. You know I intimated to you, sometime since, that I felt somewhat encouraged. The state of religious feeling has been gradually improving, for some weeks. Last Sabbath afternoon there was a violent thunderstorm, during which, as you may have heard, the lightning entered the house of Mr. Hannaford, and killed him and his wife, and a member of the institution. This event has seemed to produce a crisis in the state of feeling, and many have been anxious in each department. On Tuesday evening, about thirty were present in the upper hall of the seminary for inquiry, and on Wednesday eight ladies called upon me for religious conversation.

"Several have been anxious in our house. A few have expressed hope, and we are indulging a little hope for a few more. Professor Smith and the good brethren of the institution are attentive to our wants. We had a very solemn meeting last night, and are to devote the morrow to religious exercises. I am sure you will pray for us. Much of the excitement, doubtless, is the effect of fear or sympathy, but I do hope there will be some precious grain gathered from among the chaff.

" We have prayer meetings every morning, in the respective boarding houses, and the young ladies frequently go out to make calls. Only few are opposers. Miss Nutting has been among the anxious, and is indulging a little hope, and two or three more of our boarders also, and one of Dr. S——'s daughters. O! how much reason have we to thank the Lord for his great kindness to those so unworthy. We are destined to see a reverse soon, undoubtedly. We have done very little at study this week, and examination is drawing near. I expect in one week from this time we shall be immersed in study. I have resolved to risk the consequences of a partial suspension of our studies, lest I should be the means of staying the hand of God. It will affect our examination somewhat, I presume, but we ought not to be troubled about that.

" Aug. 4. We are all now very busy, and I am afraid you will not find much that looks like religion among us. I am not disheartened. It is what we might naturally expect. I hope, however, you will not see anything in our little sisters, (this is the appellation by which we are accustomed to designate those who have indulged hope) unbecoming the

Christian character — they appear exceedingly well. There are twenty of this interesting class. What hath God wrought! Perhaps we shall exhibit tolerably. We expect every one here almost."

She writes the first of the fall term : —

"I found things in a very bad state when I returned, at the close of my vacation — Christians coldhearted, and some of those who indulged hope last term, practically denying the Saviour. I have been obliged to reprove several very severely. Some of them have needed discipline almost every day. I have been trying gentle and conciliating measures for nearly four weeks, and very recently have had recourse to severe ones. Many have been much irritated, but the prospect is now, that all will issue in good."

In another letter ; —

"The ladies have suffered a serious declension in their religious feelings during the vacation. I was really alarmed and afflicted on Saturday and Sabbath last ; but the exercises of the Sabbath were highly appropriate, and I have since felt more encouraged. We have been endeavoring to adopt the most efficient means to preserve a consistent Christian deportment among those who profess to be pious, and hope that by the blessing of God we shall soon find ourselves in a more comfortable state. I am permitted even now to record the goodness of God ; we are again enjoying a gradual revival. Four have already indulged hope, and several are anxious. The seriousness, I hope, is increasing, and Christians' feelings more awakened. Miss N. now takes her turn in the performance of religious duties in school, and gives the fullest evidences of piety. I have not enjoyed so much in my own mind as at some former periods. I have never been so afflicted with my treacherous heart."

A little after, she says, —

"Everything is pleasant with us now, except we do not see a continuation of the work of the Lord so powerfully as we hoped. I think, however, we might expect much here from energetic and judicious efforts. But there are none ready for the work. I have myself felt, as a general thing, a great degree of languor, although I at times have enjoyed much in attempting to perform my duty. Last evening and to-day I have been unusually happy. There are several very interesting ladies who are somewhat anxious, for whom I feel very much. I seem to want them for mine. O, that God would give them to me. I love them tenderly. I feel pefectly at home now in my school. My naughty girls are coming up to their duty pretty well, and a spirit of affection seems to be cultivated. I hope at least we shall part in love. I am obliged to hold the reins a little straighter than is pleasant. I offend some almost every day. I expect if Mrs. —— was here at present, she would think, in good earnest, I knew how to scold. However, if the Misses do right there is no difficulty, but if they do wrong, they cannot expect to get on smoothly here. I do not know but I shall become generally unpopular. What then would you say?

"The gentlemen of the Institution hold me not much in favor this season — but there is no love lost,

I apprehend. We found some not quite discreet, and I thought it expedient to caution."

We see, in the extracts above, the effects of very great and sudden excitements in religious feelings. This revival was very different from those which have generally characterized the Seminary. It was not the result of conviction, but that of terror. The scene which had been witnessed, connected with the thunder storm, had, indeed, been awful, and should have impressed every one with the necessity of preparation for the solemn realities of eternity. But excitable temperaments were liable, in the general interest, to feel that they had passed from death unto life, while they were still enemies to God.

Let me not be understood to say that it is wrong to turn circumstances of such awful moment to the furtherance of the Redeemer's kingdom. Every favorable circumstance should be improved, to impress divine truth upon the sinner's mind. The heart is so prone to feel that all is well, and that future time is a good time, that in some cases nothing but a judgment from God, set home by the Spirit's energy, will break the spell, and fix the mind upon the interest of the soul. But measures should be chosen in the fear of God, and prosecuted with wisdom and discretion.

A revival in a literary institution, composed of both sexes, is exceedingly difficult to be conducted. " In Christ there is neither male nor female." In a revival there is a common interest. Young ladies and gentlemen meet as brothers and sisters — they are one — they have similar feelings, similar interests. It seems really prudish to maintain that respectful distance which characterizes other periods. But if it is dispensed with, a return to usual etiquette is not effected without serious discipline. Besides, regularity is liable to be encroached upon; studies become of secondary consequence; late hours, bad lessons, absence from school, seem to the pupil at least, the necessary attendants upon a religious excitement. But there is a surer, a better way. Wisdom should ever characterize every movement in school, where the mind is moulded for the active scenes of life, in which we are required to maintain religion in the midst of cares, perplexities, and anxieties. These are the invariable attendants of every human being. We must learn that we are sanctified but in part; and that if we would please God, if we would do good, we must pursue an even, judicious course, every moment of our lives. This truth may be impressed upon the heart when it is first given to God. Indeed this is the moment to show that it is possible to be "diligent in business, fervent in spirit, serving the Lord." And, if at the time of a revival in a public institution, all the exercises of school were required, — if there were the same watchfulness over the conduct, and the same perseverance exhibited in securing punctuality and strict propriety, the ill effects attendant upon a revival would be immediately banished. There might not be so many professed converts, — but those " called by the *name* of Israel " would be " *of* Israel."

The revival of the summer of 1833, was the only one resulting from external excitement. They were, with this exception, the result of God's blessings upon

11

the prayers and labors of his people, universally preceded by increased personal devotion and anxiety for the salvation of sinners. The one of the summer of 1834 was of this character.

Miss H. writes, June 29th : " I have been endeavoring to do my duty to-day, and although I have not been so fervent in my supplications as is required, I have felt as if I could approach God as my Father, and confidently present to him my desires. We shall be able to number a few souls among the redeemed I hope. I can speak with confidence of only one, but I feel to plead for others who are somewhat serious."

July 9th. " The brethren are just beginning to become engaged in religion. Interest increases every day — quite a number are anxious — several of my pupils have for some time been indulging a trembling hope — may these be confirmed. Many still continue to be anxious, and some are just beginning seriously to attend to the subject. I have been exerting myself so much that I am already quite exhausted. But now, by the blessing of kind Providence, the brethren are ready to assist me."

July 18th. " I have just returned from a meeting of those who are indulging hopes. There are no less than fifteen in my department, who give more or less evidence of a change of heart. Let us bless the name of the Lord for his great mercy. The young converts meet every evening at some boarding-house, and all engage personally in the devotions. They have begun to act vigorously for God. I hope they will always be characterized by practical piety."

October 1st. " I long to feel truly engaged in the work of the Lord, and to see it prosperous. I have felt much comfort in my own soul, but an unaccountable weakness in my efforts for others. More than one third of the term has already elapsed, and it is high time that we were gathering in our spiritual harvest. O, for a refreshing shower of divine grace. I have had the Presidency of the Berean Society for the month past. I am to enter the Bible class next Sabbath. O, may I have a heart to feel for them, and a tongue to persuade."

October 11th. " This has been a happy day with us. One of our number is born unto the kingdom of God. Her soul seems full of love. She can find no language to express her feelings. The brethren and the teachers of the Institution, are very anxious for the salvation of souls."

The extracts above show that the revivals at New Hampton were progressive works, preceded by unusual engagedness on the part of Christians, prosecuted with prayer and judicious effort, and followed up by initiation into the duties of a Christian. Young converts were taught to pray and labor for the promotion of the gospel of Christ, and to maintain a consistent devotional walk.

Such revivals are blessings full of mercy and free from evil. Every seminary ought, every term, to be characterized by such an outpouring of the spirit of God ; and we are fully assured, by inspiration, that if we should go forth weeping, bearing precious seed, it would result invariably in a precious harvest.

CHAPTER XIII.

THERE was a glow, an enthusiasm, a buoyancy
thrown over the correspondence of Miss H. during
1834, which characterized no other period of her life.
She was ready to every work, and made every duty
a pleasure. She spent the winter of 1834 at the Institution. She wished to retain a small class of advanced pupils, but was unable to secure board at the
village upon eligible terms, and so was obliged to obtain other accommodations. She writes to a friend
at this time — "Another bold step ! Do you believe
I have rented Professor F.'s house for a longer or
shorter time, and intend to keep a boarding house ?
I must learn to live, you know. We cannot secure
board at the village for much less than two dollars,
and this will never do."

February 1st, she writes to Miss Hadley, —

" I am very pleasantly situated for the winter in
the house formerly occupied by Professor F. — have
everything quite as well as I expected — just sixteen
scholars — every room completely filled. I should

admire to have you visit me. Miss Sleeper and I have the parlor chamber, and everything perfectly to our minds. I have never passed a winter with so little exposure of health. I have not had the least cold during the whole time. Have punctual conveyance to meeting, frequent calls from the Professors, and indeed every comfort. My privileges are far greater than formerly. Our new Professors are excellent men, and very improving to society. We have excellent preaching and good books. I am becoming very ambitious — have got hold of a new link in the chain of science, and feel constantly an eager, inquisitive spirit.

" There seems to be an increasing interest in religion among some of the brethren, and the people of the village. Several, I am told, are already cherishing hopes. I have attended meeting at the village. Professor S. preached two excellent sermons. Mr. —— was baptized, and several others will go forward next week.

" Last fall, I was ready to exclaim, 'all these things are against me.' But the Lord's ways are not as our ways. How short-sighted are we! I feel astonished that I was so disheartened. I should have felt, that though clouds and darkness were round about Him, justice and judgment are the habitations of his throne. How many lessons do we often need to impress upon us the most simple truths. I am sure I am a very untractable scholar. I have need of all the chastisement I receive, to keep me in my place — to make me, inclined as I am to feel strong and self-sufficient, know my dependence."

11*

February 7th, to Mr. Smith.

" Yesterday I attended worship at the village,
Had a sermon in the morning from this text, ' Lord,
what wilt thou have me to do ? ' At noon, four candidates received baptism. Everything was delightful.
I never saw so much love and sweet harmony in New
Hampton as seems to exist at present. The house
was full. This evening I have attended the conference ; the brethren seem like new men. I did not
suppose we had among us half of the talent which is
now exhibited. O how wonderful is the power of
religion ! While it renovates the soul, it invigorates
the mind.

Mr. Smith is soon to go to Concord with Mr.
Quincy to consult relating to the appointment of
Professors. Mr. Morse will probably become Professor of Languages, and Mr. White of Mathematics
and Natural Philosophy. You will recollect both of
the young men. They fitted for college at this Institution.

March 22. Our winter school is closed ; the
scholars have dispersed, and I am at my home. You
will want to know the result of our boarding enterprise. Very happy indeed. No circumstance has
taken place since I have been at New Hampton more
gratifying to myself. Instead of fifteen shillings or
two dollars, as was predicted by some persons interested, all expenses were less than nine shillings per
week. If ever I felt grateful, I think it was on Friday night. I have been extremely anxious at times
during the winter, observing so many eyes upon us.
They thought, I doubt not, that I had missed the

mark once in my life. But all ended well, and I feel perfectly free from anxiety."

May 11th, 1834. — To a friend.

"I am permitted still to speak of success. We have entered ninety-seven ladies, and they have a greater number at the other department. The new professors are very popular.

June 14. I have just returned from a six o'clock prayer meeting. We always meet at this hour, Saturday evening, in the upper hall, to prepare for the Sabbath. But we felt as if thrown into the straits of Thermopylæ, and it has been good for us, I trust. Christians here have seemed very indifferent thus far this term; I became quite discouraged, and resolved to turn my efforts to the younger members of the school, those not professors of religion.

Many of them are now thoughtful, and some are professed inquirers. We are, at present, suffering very much from interruption in worship on Sabbath days. The church are resolved not to have written sermons, and Professor S. does not see fit to extemporize altogether.

July 29th. Another examination is approaching. At this momentous period I am intending to rely entirely upon the resources of my own mind for everything; I shall have no books about, except in the languages, and very little paper. If I have self-command, there will be no danger, the classes are well prepared."

Previous to this time, there was not sufficient discipline on the part of the pupils to throw them upon their own resources. They required weeks and months of training to prepare them to present the knowledge which they had accumulated. There was not sufficient maturity to communicate thought, without an amount of previous labor, which rendered the examinations strongly allied to exhibitions; but from this period, examinations partook of an altogether different character, teaching was different, it was changed from general questions to rigid analysis, and the scholars reviewed, and re-reviewed, till the whole subject was completely mastered. Questions were almost entirely dispensed with. At recitations teachers had performed the labor for the pupils, now the pupils did the work and received the advantage.

From this time the school was characterized by rigid discipline, and independent acquisition; what the scholar knew, was thoroughly acquired, and ready to be communicated at any moment.

The summer vacation of 1834, Miss H. accompanied Mr. Smith to the White Mountains. A little after she thus writes to Miss Hall: —

"I am sorry I have not time this morning to write you a long letter. Miss B. will tell you all interesting particulars concerning things here. I have a multiplicity of daily cares which are sometimes oppressive, but have far more cause for gratitude than complaint. If your health would permit, and your funds were adequate, I would invite you to pass the winter with me. We shall have about sixteen select young ladies, with whose society I am sure you would be pleased. If you are calculating to teach in the spring, and your circumstances permit, I should think you had better come. Write to me at any rate.

Your respects were duly tendered to my friend. Please accept his in return. He made me a very pleasant visit in August, which we improved by taking a trip to the White Mountains. Brother Evans preached for us last Sabbath. He seems to be pleasantly situated in Canaan."

A few weeks after she writes to Mrs. Purkitt: —

" *My Dear Rebecca*, — Because you are married, or have moved to Lexington, or for some other reason, it seems our correspondence is dropped. Indeed! Now who is to blame for this, I do not know, but conclude I will venture at any rate to send a letter to Mrs. John H. Purkitt, of Lexington. Now it occurs to me, that as you are a matron lady, I must assume a grave style; but no, I shall presume you are still my old friend Rebecca. Now, what can you find to set yourself about? *Really*, do some sewing for that best friend! But then, this will not occupy but part of the time. O yes! you write now and then, as *he* is making his official tours, and read his returns more than once each, certainly, (for the lover is not lost in the husband.) You write for the treasury — go to Boston once in a while — wait on friends in return: these make out quite a list of items of business. And how pleasant! Nobody to trouble you — a kind mother and sister always ready to render you any service, and a dear husband to return now and then to gladden your heart. And what could you wish for more? Is there anything to mar your peace? Nothing *real*, I am sure, and I hope nothing imagined. These are doubtless halcyon days for you. They are as the first fruits of mature life. O then, let them be devoted as an offering to your blessed Saviour !

"You probably hear from my friend once in a while. He is in excellent health, and enjoys study. He writes that you have forwarded him a wedding card for me — thank you — shall most certainly call. All things are very well with *us* — never more so. Our board of teachers in both departments, (myself excepted of course) is as good as could be wished. No bustle, no trouble — everything moves easily. These are new times for us, you must suppose. We ought to feel gratitude to God."

She writes to Miss Patterson: — "I can truly say I am thankful to break, at length, our long, and to me, painful silence. 'The wicked shall not go unpunished.' Of this truth, I think I should have been convinced from my own experience, had I no other proof. You, doubtless, recollect the promises of reformation which I so confidently made you in my last, upon condition of receiving your forgiveness for my former neglect; but alas ! I am in fault again, more deeply than before. If you believe, however, in the doctrine of expiation by purgatory, I am sure you would consider me absolved, if I should tell you half the mental suffering I have experienced on account of it. But this would be too long a story. Suffice it to say, that I presume a single week has not passed since the reception of yours, in which my conscience has not upbraided me with my neglect. Why I have, notwithstanding all this, put off so easy and so pleasant a duty from day to day till the present time, I can give no good reason. Like those

whom Rhadamanthus placed aside, I am sure 'I
have been very busy,' and this is the most I can say.
I ought, in justice to myself however, to make a reserve of the time which has elapsed since the commencement of the present term. At that time, I
had seriously determined, let other things go as they
might, to answer your valued yet slighted letter, but
while actually on the eve of commencing, I was indirectly informed, by way of Miss B. of Bristol, that
you were very ill, in the last stages of a consumption. You can judge what were then my reflections. I endeavored, for some weeks, to obtain some
item of information, which would enable me either
to write to yourself or your friends, but without
effect, until yesterday, I received intelligence from
the post-master of Londonderry, that you were visiting at Dunbarton, and had not been seriously ill.
Presuming, therefore, upon your charity, I have resolved to write you, that I may at least have the satisfaction of confessing my fault, if I may not hope
for your forgiveness.

" You suggest, my dear friend, that you had begun
to think yourself forgotten by those you once considered your New Hampton friends. I could give
you ample assurance, that you are still remembered
here with sincere affection. In our family circle your
name is often mentioned, and always when little
gossips of old friends meet, as we sometimes do.
Days of adversity are often those upon which we
reflect with the deepest interest. Such, in some
sense, may those be regarded, in which you shared
our fortunes. Everything connected with that period

lives in our memory, and will ever live. Those who sustained me then, either directly or indirectly, will ever share my gratitude.

"You ask me, humorously, concerning a picture which I sometimes wear under my belt. I suppose we always feel a secret pleasure in speaking to friends, of those, we love, but as others cannot be presumed to partake of our partialities, it is generally wisdom to say but little here. I do, indeed, enjoy the pleasures of friendship, and though chastened by absence, distance and protracted hope, I feel its solace. Still, I think the earth sets loosely about me, and were I fit for heaven, I should almost wish to soar away."

CHAPTER XIV.

In 1834, Miss Hazeltine was still discussing the expediency of becoming a missionary. She writes, in a letter to Mr. Smith, January 2d: "I have, sometimes the past week, thought much upon the subject of missions. I hear and read respecting missionaries, and often feel a peculiar thrill at the mention of the subject. From the tone of your last letter, I expect your feelings have corresponded with my own. But your plan of going to Hamilton, at present, I think would be decidedly wrong. And, if you will allow me to assume the dictatorial style, I will give you my reasons. You say you wish we might be able to improve this privilege, as brother Wade is now professor of Burman at Hamilton. I do indeed. Happy the favored few! But we are not ready. It would be certainly wrong for you, as, whatever attention you might bestow upon Burman, would be so much subtracted from your regular literary course. Yet, independent of this consideration, the uncertainty of your ever engaging in missionary labor, or, if so, of being destined for Burmah, would be nearly conclu-

12

sive. Besides, the board will, undoubtedly, have a professorship before long, so that we should be provided for, should Providence call us to that field.

"You spoke, in your last, of not doing much good where you are. I have been oppressed with this feeling very much lately, and this, in part, has given rise to my uneasiness relative to missions. I feel, however, more encouraged this week. I hope you will not allow yourself to despond. This is with you, specially, a season of preparation.

"Jan. 6. This is the evening when, so many, in Christian lands, are engaged in prayer, for the conversion of the world. I presume you are thus engaged. We have passed the day in public prayer, at the village. In the morning, prayers were offered for the progress of religion in the town, and in the afternoon, for the success of missions. I have wept to day, so forcibly have former impressions been revived in my mind. O, that I were in heart, as much elevated as I once was! I have serious doubts, whether I ought ever to become a missionary. But I feel that the spirit of missions, and the spirit of religion, are inseparably connected in relation to myself. I am inclined to think that I might be more useful at home than on heathen ground, while others, who would do less at home, would do as much abroad. But when I relinquish thoughts of a missionary life, I seem to fall into a stupid frame. This may be accounted for, however, upon philosophical principles. I hope I shall come to feel that I have sufficient motives to prompt me to a holy life, aside from the missionary enterprise. Should we become missionaries, we must sacrifice everything. But I should prefer to do this rather than be conformed to the world. I do not think I shall ever sustain a mediocrity of condition. But I would not anticipate evil. I will trust in God, and pray that he will prepare me to be useful in whatever condition he may place me. Perhaps I shall be glad to retire from the anxieties of public labor, and find a refuge in the dear delights of domestic life. Such anticipations, *sometimes*, seem bliss to me, and if I were not afraid of the fatal effects upon my piety, I should certainly cherish them. But we must remember that all flesh is grass. 'The grave is near the cradle scene.' These melancholy lines, in your melancholy air, pass through my mind, whenever I feel inclined to rest in earthly hopes. O, let us soar above them! Let us strive to fix our anchor in heaven!"

Jan. 28, she writes to the same: —

"I am apprehensive that you were sad, when you wrote last. If I had seen you, I am inclined to think I should have endeavored to remove those gloomy vapors from your brow. My letter must have been a miserable comforter. I was suffering from darkness of mind, from a bitter consciousness of sin reigning within me. I have felt similarly for most of the time since. Yesterday, in particular, I could but abhor myself. My only hope was, that the blood of Christ is able to wash away the greatest guilt. In this view I found some relief. I have never supposed that so much wickedness was in my heart, as I have recently discovered there. If this discovery should make me humble, I should have reason to bless the Lord, notwithstanding the pain it causes me. I feel much happier to-day, though I still regard myself as a loathsome being. I feel as if I never could lift up my head in the presence of God. My best motives, I have reason to regard, as either ambitious, or selfish, and am ready to question, whether there was ever the least holy principle implanted in my heart. But I will confess my sin, and thankfully believe that the blood of Jesus Christ cleanses from all sin. I presume you have similar trials. Let us be comforted, for although exceedingly vile, the grace of God is sufficient for us. Christ came to save the chief of sinners. As such, let us go to him, and he will kindly support us. He chasteneth us for our profit.

"I am afraid I wrote in my last letter what I ought not. I spoke of myself, perhaps, too much, in relation to our ultimate destination. But I spoke only in relation to the corruptions of my wicked heart, and the influence high hopes, not realized, would have upon the character. I have no anxiety respecting the field of our future labors. I am glad you still hold yourself ready to go whither Providence may lead. May the Lord enable me to comfort and assist you."

She writes to the same in February : — " I have been much happier since I wrote you last. I have had some sense of spiritual things. I have seemed to exercise some faith in prayer — have found it good to lay hold of the promises — have felt very earnestly to pray for the conversion of this people, and have thirsted for large measures of grace and entire conformity to the likeness of God. O, that I might continually have hungerings and thirstings after right-eousness, so that I might claim the promise. Nor has the friend of my heart been forgotten. I cannot tell you how deeply interested I feel for your spiritual prosperity. My prayer is, that you may be full of the Holy Ghost. O, that we were like the holy Apostles! — so fully given to the work of God, so deeply imbued with the blessed Gospel! O, let us strive for it — for this let us earnestly beseech the Lord !

" I am very glad your Bible class seems interested. I hope the Lord will make you wise to win souls — that he will encourage your heart, by permitting you to be instrumental in bringing sinners to repentance. Still labor and pray. Expect great things ; attempt great things ; and may the Lord make you to realize your largest desires. I trust he will, when he sees you sufficiently humble to bear it. I am happy to hope that you do not permit your affection for me to interfere with any of your duties. I hope I may live in your memory and in your heart without drawing you into a snare. May the Lord sanctify our affec-tion ! "

March 7. To the same : —

" If God should spare your life, and give you health satisfactorily to complete your studies, should he nour-ish the tender plant of affection, and at length unite our hearts, what would we not render to him ! What but ourselves, sacredly, and for ever. This we will do ; we will be the Lord's. I am very happy in prayer for the extension of the Redeemer's kingdom. I feel as if it were not a vain thing to call upon the

12*

Lord. I hope I do love him, and love his cause, though I am not so entirely under the influence of the Gospel as I ought to be.

"The death of Mr. Rostan is a severe affliction. How will Zion mourn! Poor France, who will care for her! who labor for her salvation! If I were competent, I should love to go to France. But I do not know how I should meet their subtle logic. Indeed I am not prepared to go anywhere. I am a mere infant in knowledge. You speak of China. I could find no place there. I believe ladies are not admitted. It would be very hard, indeed, to go alone among the heathen. This would be a trying case. Have either of us grace enough to do this, were it necessary? Nought but a great, a very great change, would enable me to go single-handed into distant heathen climes. But I feel as if I could go with a friend, if God should call. Do you think that your constitution will ever allow you to go to a warm climate?"

To the same, July 18: —

"I hardly think it will do for you to think of ever leaving New England. You are so much affected by dampness; and you know there is scarcely a place in the world, where there is not more wet weather than here. I should not suggest such a thought, did I not fear the effect of an ultimate disappointment upon this subject. The hope of engaging, personally, in the missionary enterprise, has been a continual stimulus to me until somewhat recently. Since I have felt my expectations in some degree checked, I have often found an inclination in myself to sink down inactive. But since I have made up my mind to stay at home, if Providence may seem so to dictate, and have been somewhat disposed to think that this may probably be my destiny, I have felt a renewal of my energies. But the Lord must dispose of us, I know not in what manner, nor ought I to be anxious. I feel prepared to go, if it seems duty. But I am afraid your life would be very short, either in an eastern or western country."

CHAPTER XV.

WERE idle curiosity alone to be gratified by a view
of the period in the life of Miss. H., which we are
now approaching, we would pass it in silence. But
we write to do good, and with this specific design,
we shall attempt a true delineation.

There are few long and intimate acquaintances,
previous to marriage, uninterrupted. " The course
of true love never did run smooth." But while
thousands have felt the bitterness of a misunderstanding, and all its attendant evils, and the world
has been no wiser, in the instance which we are now
contemplating, the result was altogether different.
Miss Hazeltine occupied a public position — had
devoted herself to the cause of Christ — this act
could not fail to exert its influence on the religion
she professed. All trembled for the effect, and most
believed, that though her previous history had been
marked by uprightness, this was a stain, which could
not be easily removed. It was certainly a very
unfortunate step. This, and its attendant circumstances, changed the previous happy tenor of her

life, to one of bitterness, undermined her constitution, and sent her to an early grave. But it naturally resulted from the peculiar elements of her character, and the influence of her condition. Though the step was unfortunate, yet, it is to be regarded, principally, if not entirely, as her misfortune rather than as her fault. Though her decision proved to be unwise, yet, all who knew her, believe it to have been conscientious.

If the hope of a missionary life had never been surrendered, she would probably have continued her engagement with Mr. Smith. She could never endure the thought of a quiet, unimportant existence. Leisure was wretchedness — care and responsibility, her greatest pleasure. We have already referred to her strong desire to secure the approbation of God, and the regard of the wise and good. In her own public career, she gratified these impulses of her nature. She found scope for every energy — had a consciousness of distinguished usefulness, and was generally esteemed. And she felt that her happiness required their continuance.

When she commenced correspondence with Mr. Smith, it was not with reference to personal feelings alone. She asked if, in this course, she should receive the blessing of Heaven, and the approbation of friends, and decided that could these be secured, she should be happy in its consummation. It had been expected that Mr. Smith would become a missionary, and Miss Hazeltine felt, that by connection with him, she could command a more extensive field of usefulness than the one she now occupied. Now,

she educated those, who, independent of her assistance, might secure every advantage of literary and
religious instruction. In the sphere in which she
moved, there was a greater proportion of teachers
than of pupils. But in a missionary field the scene
was different. Millions must there for ever remain
destitute of the bread of life, because there is no one
to lead them in the right path. It was also, in her
view, labor fraught with an amount of self-denial and
difficulty, which gave it a rank highest among human
efforts.

She felt, when the engagement was made, that, in
her decision, she should receive the approbation of
her friends. While Mr. Smith was disconnected
with herself, and regarded without any reference to
becoming the partner of so distinguished a lady, she
believed that he stood so well in community, that
her own fame would not be lessened by a personal
connection. But when the decision was once made,
the universal silence in community was a dagger to
her heart. She no longer had a free expression of
public opinion. Mr. Smith, independently considered, and Mr. Smith, the special friend of Miss
Hazeltine, were very different individuals. The pol-
itic world did not heartily acquiesce in her choice.
This alone, with her sensitive nature and high esteem
for the opinion of friends, was enough to cause her
to vacillate. She feared she might have hoped too
much for him. She doubted whether he did actually possess those brilliant talents, which would command a place that she could fill with honor and usefulness. Had these considerations been before her

mind, before she gave Mr. S. an affirmative answer, perhaps her affections might not have become so identified with their beloved object, as to prevent her usefulness and happiness in some other sphere. But she decided otherwise. She allowed her affections to flow forth in all their fulness. All her thoughts and plans had their spring in this one source. When the consideration above came to bear, she felt that her affections would not allow her to change her purpose. This fact, and the hope that the community would finally sanction her decision, and maturity render him all her aspirings would ask, induced her to continue the engagement. When under the influence of her own judgment only, her path of duty seemed plain, and her feelings decided.

She knew that Mr. Smith was not only a man of integrity, but of ardent piety — not only that he was susceptible of ardent affection, but that it was all hers, and from the nature of his character, would continue so for ever. She knew he was alive to the blessings of domestic life — would appreciate all her little wants, and every feeling of a heart overflowing with kindly emotion. This was all her affections demanded. Had she felt that she could resign public celebrity to possess the affection and contribute to the happiness of one she so devotedly loved, her feelings, and the tenor of her life might have continued undisturbed. But her ruling desire was, to be connected with Mr. Smith, and to have him become all that was commanding in the eye of the public, and in her own fancy.

The tenor of her letters to him were such as to

prompt to effort for the greatest possible excellence. In one of them she says: "I know that however unworthy I may be, I never could be satisfied with a companion who did not stand high in his profession. You must not presume upon my love. I must not presume upon it; if you are not to be a minister, (for it is only upon this point there can be any question,) with whom I may be rationally pleased, I am decided, that it would be a duty, which we owe each other, to relinquish all thoughts of a future union. But should Heaven permit you to pursue the course of study which you contemplate, I am persuaded I shall find in you all I could ask as a minister, a friend, and a companion."

In another letter she writes: "You ask, if I think people generally believe our correspondence to be injudicious on my part. I do not think those, for whom I ought to care, think so. Still, I cannot say, I am not affected by what any one says relating to yourself. I feel a word, or even silence, to the very heart. What has been said, as far as has come to my knowledge, affects not at all my opinion of your merit. I have been distrustful of my own decision, and have been led sometimes to query, whether my judgment was not influenced by feelings of partiality."

Miss Hazeltine felt, that when she became a wife, she must resign her individual character, and live in her husband; but could he become all her bright imaginings could picture, she would be content to bask in the radiance of his fame. And why could not Mr. Smith be all this? He would have all the advantages of a liberal education, he would, in all probability, be a missionary, and certainly that bespoke him of no ordinary mould. Time passed. She hoped, yet she feared, doubted. She knew his constitution was not perfectly vigorous. This, and other circumstances to which we have alluded, led her to feel that the missionary enterprise must be surrendered, and this surrendered, she felt an increased desire to be associated with one of distinguished talents. The question now became, not, can I do without, but can I always be happy with. The year before the engagement was dissolved, necessary circumstances rendered a personal interview impracticable. This perhaps to some extent unpleasantly affected the feelings.

The letters, we have presented, develop the circumstances under which her engagement had been made, and the principles, upon which it had been continued. Miss Hazeltine always said that she should watch the intimations of Providence, and hold herself responsible to abide by its decisions. She now felt that the relation which they had sustained to each other, the two preceding years, ought to be dissolved. She proposed this to Mr. Smith. He, for her sake, acquiesced in her decision, and, as far as possible, to shield from blame, agreed to say to the public, "*it is a mutual measure*," and that they would henceforth sustain to each other the character of kind, sympathetic friends, and nothing more. This occurred in the spring of 1835.

We sport with those who are forming connections that are to terminate only with existence. We throw our influence indifferently, and make the period of courtship a period for anything but sober reflection and candid, unbiased judgment. Had we the least glimpse of the momentous event pending, we should tread as on the most perilous ground. When we have said a woman loves, we have told her chief history. Her life is but a tale of the affections. Heaven designed her to love, and if her love is judiciously bestowed, fully returned, and properly controlled, it becomes a powerful motive to action, an ever-present object of thought, an unfailing source of pleasure. But the one permitted to lay bare the female heart, knows of anguish from misfortune in either of these respects, which would else be inconceivable.

Woman is called capricious; she indeed seems so in matters of the heart; she loves, she will love, and nothing can hinder. Let us not be misunderstood. We would not say that love arises independent of excellences of character, or that it will be maintained without their existence. But the degree, and kind of excellence to command affection, cannot be fully decided, but by the heart of the one where it is excited. Parents cannot select companions who will render their children blessed. Friends cannot, with impunity, make, or break matches. This is a matter of individual responsibility, and the criteria of judgment comparatively few. Whether there will be a splendid home, to which we shall be proud to invite friends, whether the world will smile and approve, and our vanity be gratified, are considerations relatively not worth a thought. The feelings must be examined. Will my affections there find a home? Do I esteem the object within my grasp altogether worthy? Are there those traits of character which would render affection safe and permanent? Will Heaven approve? Affection, and the characteristics which will secure its permanency, are the only safe condition for forming the engagement of marriage, and a want of these requisites, the only just argument for dissolving an engagement already formed.

If ambition, the love of fame, the desire of the world's approbation, or the world's wealth, be allowed to control our action, misfortune and wretchedness will be the inevitable result. The violation of plighted vows will cry to heaven. God seems more uniformly in this life to have punished this sin than any other. It has passed into a proverb, that unfaithful lovers will never prosper.

But God will bless any measure which his cause really requires. Besides there is that, in the character of God, which, to the upright heart, will be all that the richest affections can demand. The entire affections of the soul find scope for exercise in his perfect character, and his cause in the world may command all the sympathy prompted by affection. The heart, too, that feels a consciousness of rectitude, will express it in the carriage and conduct, and thus win friends who will occupy the thoughts, interest the feelings, and become a centre for pleasant associations, objects where the imagination may ever find exercise and repose.

A conscientious person would not, however, easily forget those who had once called forth the rich affec-

tions of the heart. This is only secured by persevering effort. There must be, for a time, the entire
banishment of the loved object. A continuation of
correspondence even, will naturally result in ill effects.
They have been lovers. The same fuel, which first
enkindled the flame, will still sustain it. Those who
have loved, cannot possibly, at will, change the feelings to those of friendship. The thought of being
still permitted to hold friendly intercourse — of cherishing the remembrance of each other — of cultivating a holy, elevated affection, might, in anticipation, seem perfectly delightful, but the result would
prove its impossibility. The sensitive heart could
not endure the necessary change of language. Epistolary correspondence so imperfectly communicates
thought, that each individual, alive to every shade of
meaning, would, through the imperfection of this
medium, almost necessarily misconstrue, and, more
than all, while correspondence was sustained, there
would be at least the shadow of a shade of hope,
which would produce constant suspense.

Those, who cease to be lovers, need not become
enemies. It is not a truth, that ardent affection be-
gets bitter hate. When one has loved with the
heart he will not hate the object once loved, nor
even seek its injury. Blind, grovelling passion may.
But the heart loves on, loves ever — seeks the good
of the loved object, and rejoices in its happiness.

CHAPTER XVI.

CONTINUES CORRESPONDENCE WITH MR. SMITH.

WHEN the engagement between Miss H. and Mr. S. was discontinued, nothing was said of continuing correspondence. But when, a few weeks after, Miss Hazeltine was bereaved by the death of her mother, Mr. Smith, in the capacity of a friend, renewed the correspondence. For a while it was uninterruptedly continued, and partook of all the tenderness and affection which had previously characterized it. The following breathes the sentiments of the whole: "Will you permit me for a few moments to love you and be happy. These are days of darkness and sorrow. What is the world to me? Nothing, absolutely nothing. When I reason upon my situation, and future prospects, I am convinced I have much for which to be thankful, and no cause for complaint; but I find it impossible to divest myself of the impression, that all is lost. Genial suns, gentle moons, verdant fields, and smiling faces are all nothing to me! My affections embrace no living object, unless it be my poor broken-hearted father, and my dear, forsaken one. O shall I say it? Weep not, my friend, I will quench

13*

my own tears. They flow but too often, when memory brings me back the treasure of my heart.

"I have no resting place for my tired imagination. If she attempts to alight for a moment, she is cruelly driven from her perch, and forced to flutter still without design in chaotic space, or take refuge in oblivion. Such are my feelings daily. I sometimes feel a little energy, as I do this evening, but it is soon spent. And yet I can study with very good effect. This is matter of astonishment to me. But I have reason to be unfeignedly thankful that it is so. I have a class in the Epistle to the Romans, one in Butler's Analogy, and another in Wayland's Philosophy, besides Latin, French, &c. The classes seem to be getting along well. The trustees meet on the coming week to deliberate on the best means to be taken to secure us eligible premises.

"I hope you are feeling more happy than I am; I have reason to think you are. I hope to feel happier after some changes shall have taken place in our situation. Things are too quiet. I want something exciting; some fine scheme ahead, or some enterprise going forward, or else everything seems to me becalmed. I feel to-night quite cheerful; perhaps because conversing with you irrespective of the topic.

"We are trying to awaken some feeling in ourselves, and in our pupils upon the subject of religion; we have but little encouragement at present. Will you not pray for us sometimes? I often pray for you with the same ardor as heretofore. May the Lord bless you abundantly henceforth and forever."

She writes to the same July 31 : —

"After the bustle and toil of the day, at half past ten o'clock, I embrace a few moments to reply to your last kind letter. You are now in the midst of your vacation; full of business, however, I apprehend. May the best of blessings, the presence and comfort of Jehovah, continually make your heart to rejoice. I am trying to take fast hold of his treasures; they are rich, and boundless, and free for all who seek them aright. I sometimes obtain such views of the excellence of spiritual joys, that I am ready to surrender cheerfully all of an earthly nature, which my heart has cherished. But alas, I am human; and cannot break the cords which bind me to earth. 'He knoweth our frame, he remembereth that we are dust.'

"I am very sorry indeed that I have been so foolish as to complain to you so much; I might have known it was improper, but I had nowhere else to go. You were enjoying tranquillity of mind, and I seemed to chide you; forgive me this wrong. It is true I have been sad, *very* sad; but still I must not yield the dictates of reason, to the yearnings of affection. I have generally felt much more cheerful for the last four weeks than before. I have had a few seasons of mental conflict, but have generally soon become calm. You must not feel concerned about me. I dare say I shall obtain the victory, if God will grant me his precious aid. And I feel to hope he will; I think he does sometimes. Do not be troubled about me; I am now perfectly well, and I presume, the girls think I am in great spirits. All the folks are very kind, Mr. and Mrs. Smith, in particular.   I am very much interested in my studies, hope to feel confidence in examining them.   I am willing to have my classes questioned as much as they please; intend to have the assignments made in the languages, or anywhere else, by the visiters.   I begin to have renewed confidence in myself as a teacher; have been thinking to-day that this is probably my calling.   Do you think 1 can be contented in it?   Had I a dear friend by my side, to whom I could look up, I think I could devote myself to teaching as long as 1 live, with the greatest delight.   But probably you do not wish to hear any more about *me*, that is from my pen; O how dear is self to self!   Nothing so dear, except self reflected in friendship's mirror.   Friendship!   O, how dear a word!   Friendship!   precious boon!   now doubly dear.   Friendship — it is the only earthly boon I crave.   O my friend, may this precious boon be yours.   May you taste all its sweets unmingled.

" Be peaceful, be happy.   *Your* sun has not set; rejoice in its glory.   Heaven bless thee, dearest, with its choicest gifts.   O could 1 make you happy! — But there is One who can.   Avail yourself of his friendship; he will never disappoint you.   ' There's *nothing true* but Heaven.' "

She writes to Mrs. P. July 17 : —

" As to my feelings, Rebecca, I have no time to feel.   I feel as usual.   I dare say you have thought of me with some solicitude; and I have seen many times, when it would have given me great pleasure to have enjoyed a friendly chat with you, and to have engaged your sympathy.   But all is well, in every respect, so far as I know.   I hope to see you in August, and to commune with you upon many things, concerning which I cannot so well write.   But you may be assured I have no anxiety, except for the success of my examination.   We expect a great deal of company, and I am sure I do not know what they are coming to see, unless it be 'a reed shaken by the wind.'"

She writes to Miss H. H. Smith, in August, from Boston : —

"Your affectionate letter was most gratefully received.   It came at a time when I needed a cordial, and a cordial it truly was.   You will never know, I trust, the emotions which *I* have known — I cannot speak of them, and yet I know not how to speak of anything else.   I have often sat in mute amazement, verifying the language of the poet, 'be *these lips* in *holy silence sealed.*'   My favorite posture has been that of my elbow upon the table, and my fingers upon my lips.   All his waves and his billows have gone over me.   But sorrow like this is *consumption;* it drinketh up the spirits.   I am endeavoring to feel calm and resigned, that the remainder of my life may, at least, pass quietly away.   What the future will develop is unknown to me ; and I am willing it should be so.   If I can but pursue such a course as God shall approve, it *should* be, and I hope *is*, my chief concern.   My dear Hannah, I am very sorry that your health is so poor.   I am concerned for you, for my dear Joseph's sake.   You will comfort him.   He has been wonderfully sustained, but he will need a friend.   You will ever cleave to him with the utmost

fondness and faithfulness, I feel assured. Love him
for my sake, and may he be a comfort to you. Do
not feel anxious about us. I feel gloomy to-day, but
I think God will support us both, and will so order
events that our happiness and usefulness will be most
effectually secured, if we do not distrust him. Be
sure not to trouble yourself about us; all, I trust,
will be well. Take the best possible care of your
health, and endeavor to fix your hopes firmly in Heaven. All below the sun is fading and uncertain;
'there's nothing true but *Heaven.*' How often have
I felt inclined to dispute this sentiment. In one sense
it is *not* true; but in the sense chiefly intended, it is
true. Hannah, lay *fast hold* on *Heaven,* otherwise,
the billows of adversity may bear you away. See
that your anchor is cast *sure.* I wish I could see
you; we would mingle our tears, would prudence
permit. But 'there is a calm for those who weep,'
and in the anticipation of that peaceful rest, I often
lay down my head.

"I feel very gloomy to-day — I have walked to
meeting by my brother's side, but sustained by no
kind arm. It is all well, however. I had not the
pleasure of being introduced to the lady by whom you
sent your letter; regret it very much. Please make
my regards to her, if you think proper. My affectionate regards also to sister Carr, and to your friends as
you have opportunity. I feel no less interest in yourself and in them, be assured, than heretofore. Joseph
intends to visit you to-morrow, and I hope he will
call when he returns, and let me know how you do.
So long as *he* regards me as a friend, may I not hope
you will regard me so also?"

She writes to Mr. Smith September 10: —

"Your letter has been received to-day, and produced such feelings in my mind as you might easily anticipate. I could hardly realize that it was dictated by the heart of my dear J. I could bear anything but that you should blame me. I have not felt conscious of doing wrong. I have thought I had acted towards you as I should wish you to act in like circumstances. I have done only as I thought my duty to *you*, no less than to myself required. I had no wish for any arrangement which you could not approve. I hold myself, responsible for all my engagements, if it is your wish. I should do it cheerfully, yea more, joyfully, for it would not only meet all the wishes of my heart, but I should then think it duty, and the path of duty is ever a safe and happy course. Am I responsible for my involuntary and unavoidable thoughts and feelings? Was it not my duty to communicate them to you? Could I have done otherwise, honestly? I told you I would do what was right; if you could not agree with me, I would agree with you. I love you as truly, as sincerely, and as respectfully as ever. I have somewhat withdrawn my thoughts from you, but not my affection. I am grieved that you should think hard of me, that you should find it necessary to convict me of want of integrity. I cannot divine who has influenced your mind so much against me; but it is in vain for me to say anything in self-defence. I certainly should not have expressed one word to any one, had I suspected it would injure you in the least, and had I not been in a manner compelled to do it by an extreme anxiety to know my duty."

Sept. 25. "When I received your letter, I was coming to think quite hard of you — had contrasted your former magnanimity with some things more recent, which seemed to me ungenerous, and felt inclined to sit down as one injured, and resign myself to my misfortune. I remembered that you had told me, in the days of our early acquaintance, that if you thought I should prefer any other one to yourself, you would secure my alliance with him, if it were in your power; and that since we parted last spring you have written me something like this, that you would try to pray that I might find some friend worthy, not only of my *love* but of my *confidence*. But I was led to query, whether disinterested attachment and exalted principle might come in for so large claims upon the empire of your mind, as I had supposed. Besides, I thought if you had known the principles which had actuated me in wishing our correspondence to be discontinued, you would not have opposed so serious a barrier to our friendship. Whenever I have mentioned the subject, it has been with the hope that my views might be objected to, and corrected; never, 'in my *own defence*,' much less, 'to injure you.' "

It will be seen, by the extracts above, that there was now a misunderstanding between Miss H. and Mr. S. This was commenced by communicating the circumstances to friends. An incident never lessens its importance either in our own estimation or of others, by being clothed in language. Indeed, I think experience proves, that some things, which would have resulted in infinite sorrow, by being communicated, have vanished into thin air, when retained in the bosom where they originated. This is frequently the case in our every-day intercourse. Perhaps, with a friend that is ever by our side, something occurs which excites our jealousy, something which seems to betoken a want of kind feeling, which seems really ungenerous, or even base. We should tread lightly under such circumstances, and not for the world communicate our feelings to a third, or even hastily to the seeming aggressor. We should put the best construction upon the act, and believe, if possible, that there is some other side which would reveal the mystery.

We are accused. Still let us be exceedingly cautious. Let the accusation remain with ourselves. We have then only one to convince that the whole is a mistake, and this can best be done, and perhaps only done effectively, by seeming to feel that all will certainly terminate well — that we feel a consciousness of innocence — that nothing was farther from our hearts, and that our future course will prove it so. There is nothing like forbearance to restore a waning confidence. A calm, quiet way of taking a thing, reduces mountains to molehills, and molehills to their original dust. We should hope, trust, believe, and banish every suspicion, as long as we can have the least good reason, and even when demonstration is against us, in a majority of instances, forbearance and kindness will originate the very traits which we most desire.

Let a contrary course be pursued; let blame be expressed with all the vividness which the heart, rendered feelingly alive by strong affection, sometimes realizes; let not only the aggressor be blamed, but counsellors be called in — counsellors summoned — how the wrong will magnify by the increased light thrown around it! The evil seems illimitable. If it was small at commencement, in time it becomes insurmountable.

This was the effect of communicating the circumstances that led to the dissolution of their engagement. It was agreed, when the engagement ceased, that the reasons should not be communicated. But telling tried friends was not violating the *spirit* of the condition. So Miss H. reasoned. On the other hand Mr. S. considered it as exhibiting a want of integrity, especially, as in the very nature of the case, it would be impossible for one party alone duly to present all the facts in their exact, relative importance. This was the misunderstanding. Friends, on both sides, were called in judgment, various opinions were formed, and the evil increased.

CHAPTER XVII.

SHE writes to Mr. and Mrs. F., September 18 : — " At
this solemn hour, this hour, when retiring from the
toils of the weary day, we are wont to retreat for
succor and repose to the bosom of friends; this hour,
long since to me *doubly sacred*, NOW crowded with
the tenderest reminiscences of the past, may I presume to hold converse with you, as with kindred
spirits? Will you refuse me your sympathy? Let
me, dear friends, claim this indulgence. My spirit
is like a broken reed; deal kindly with me. Your
letter was very kind; your propositions generous;
accept my sincere thanks for both. But I have no
spirit of enterprise. Forgive me then, if I cannot
leave my humble home, for prospects to *others*, and
once to *me*, alluring. I have thought I should like
to visit Providence, and on some accounts it has
seemed a desirable place, both for a residence and a
school; but in view of events which have recently
transpired, I could not go there even for a visit. I
have had causes of grief, since I saw you, altogether

unknown before. Shall I say, my dearest friend has been grieved with me — that he has suspected me of ungenerous motives! Let me tell you all my sorrows. This has been the *bitterest* cup of all. True, in some sense I had resigned my friend, but *never, as a friend.* I was willing he should place his affections on some one better calculated to render him happy than myself; but I could not bear that he should turn away from *me* with *disapprobation.* Alas, that the invidious tongue of falsehood must infuse its poison into a stricken heart, awaken jealousy in the most confiding bosoms, and alienate *very friends!* This is, however, what I might have expected; and yet I *did not* expect it. But it is all well. I still survive, and can I but devote the remainder of my days to God, it is all I crave. I know my treasure has been on earth; for my heart has been here. This bereavement is, perhaps, the only way by which I could be weaned from terrestrial hopes, and made to give my energies to God. I bless his name for afflictions. I feel to kiss the rod. My soul is subdued ; may it ever be at the feet of my Saviour."

She writes to Mrs. P. : — " Mr. Smith believes that I am calculating for myself at his expense, and of course cannot feel kindly towards me. I cannot think I am to blame, and yet, I think it is a very hard case, and have felt very much troubled. There never would have been a misunderstanding, I am persuaded, but for the unkind interference of others. And now you cannot do me any good that I know, but do write me, and confirm my resolution, if you think I am right. People are speaking very well of

Mr. S. at present. I am persuaded the impression is going against me."

Miss H. had ever, till now, regarded public sentiment as generous, and she had had reason. Few, *very few* are more highly appreciated in the circle.in which they move. Perhaps the fancied change was rather with her than with the public. It is said, that in success all claim a right to honor, but in misfortune, none acknowledge responsibility. It is equally true, that the unfortunate feel inclined to look beyond the natural tendency of their own conduct, to some unhappy interference. Miss H. felt, that she had acted conscientiously, that she ought to be happy and prosperous, and she therefore felt inclined to attribute her wretchedness to the errors of others, rather than to her own. She now for the first time felt from the heart, that this is a wicked, meddling, fickle world. She was a Christian, and knew that the human heart was exceedingly perverse. But the knowledge, to which I refer, was of another nature, and of another tendency. A knowledge of the universal depravity of man, of his sad, fallen state, leads us to commiserate, to thirst to reclaim, while individual acts of wickedness lead to misanthropy, distrust, and despair.

That mankind are treacherous in this sense, is rendered credible only by personal experience. While the world uses us well, no one can convince us that there is not goodness, disinterestedness, and constancy there. Our own experience gives the lie to a contrary assertion. *Goodness* — why every moment is rich with proof that those, upon whom we have no claims, find their greatest pleasure in contributing to our happiness. There is such a delicacy too in the carriage of those around us. True, they feel interested in knowing all we do — they give a ready ear to all our plans and hopes; but it is because they love us, and feel interested in all that relates to our success and happiness. And as to *trusting*, we know of no one in the circle of our acquaintance, in whom we could not, if circumstances required, place all our interest, with the utmost confidence.

That this is but a pleasing dream, is learned at different periods of life. Some, in early childhood, are made to weep bitter, *bitter* tears, over wicked, human nature. The buds of hope, in the spring-time of existence, have been blasted by the untimely frosts of unkindness, and as a consequence, there could be no anticipation of the flowers of summer, the rich fruit of autumn, or the full storehouse, for the ease and quiet of the winter of life. But seldom, *very seldom*, is hope so crushed, that there is not ecstasy from the anticipated joys of youth, the glory of manhood, and the ease and plenty of declining age.

The world loves to bestow favors on the young. And until the splendor of a brilliant career bursts upon its astonished vision, and arouses the envy and malice of the less successful, it is seldom, that the aspirant for its good wishes and honors, learns that he serves a fickle race — that, if one can be found bold enough to throw the first stone, the perverse nature of the multitude will not be appeased, till they have undermined the reputation, sapped the base of happiness, and doomed the disappointed aspirant to an ignominious remembrance, or early forgetfulness.

Some are, however, permitted to pass successfully this fiery ordeal. In childhood they dreamed of the pleasures of youth. A proud laurel seemed to await them as the reward of a lofty aim amid future scenes of conflict and hope. Time passed, and their bright imaginings were more than realized. They had dreamed a delicious dream, and it had been all fulfilled. These believed the asseverations of the multitude to be false. They know from experience that mankind love the ways of integrity and virtue — that they find their happiness in noble generosity and persevering constancy.

Such have not fully completed the demonstration. Let them wait till a change of circumstances shall prove that it was really the goodness, the generosity and constancy of the world, that had brought such a cloud of noble supporters, or, whether it had resulted from less virtuous qualities. Let the intellect, that in the vigor of youth gave power to serve, become imbecile from age, or, let the thirst for something new seek its gratification, the scene will immediately change. "A fickle, inconstant world," is bitterly reiterated by the votary of worldly honor. "There is, indeed, nothing true, in depraved, human nature."

But there is a more unfortunate disappointment. Some, questioning the decisions of their own judgment, or, desiring to be aided in the path of duty, consult the wisdom of the world. Mankind always have their sentiments, but they are not always founded upon principle, and hence cannot be always permanent in their nature. They can tell what *they think*, but they cannot see the heart, the feelings and the character of him they advise, and of course, can only counsel at random. The result too often proves, that the judgment of the world is fallacious, interested and inconstant.

Some lean on the world, unknowingly, and are pierced to the heart. They have prayed for direction, and even believed that they were acting from high and holy principles, while the known sentiments of others were creating an unfortunate bias. They pray God to direct them in the right path. They seek his will, yet, unknown to themselves, other motives direct their course. They act from a supposed sense of duty, and find, too late, that God had not the throne in their hearts. Even under such circumstances, however, all things will work together for good, to those who have acted sincerely. The circumstances that develop the real state of the heart, may be the only means that will issue in an entire consecration to God. Yet the pain will, none the less, be suffered.

Miss Hazeltine's sentiments of the world we learn from the following letter to a friend. She says, " I am in good spirits, excepting that I am coming to feel, that this is a very wicked world. I scarcely know where to look for good faith. There is so much *managing*, so much good policy among men esteemed the best, that one can scarcely be sure, at any time, that he is not in the midst of traitors. I have experienced no personal wrongs from any one with whom I am connected, but do not feel an assurance that I might not be a subject of injury, should circumstances of trial exist. In fact, converse with any three men, separately and confidentially, and if you do not convict every one of them of duplicity, I shall think the man who escapes deserves to be especially noticed. I am truly disgusted with the baseness which characterizes our times."

In another she says : " I cannot tell you how much I am obliged to you for your kindness of the 30th ultimo, although some of its disclosures were of a nature truly painful. It has made me less wretched, however, than it would have done, had I not entertained a slight suspicion for several months, and of consequence been, in some measure, prepared for your announcement. Though I am very sensible to faithlessness in friendship, and might, at other times, have wept bitterly at the facts you communicate, yet, through the kind support of my Heavenly Father, and the sweet balm of conscious innocence and integrity, I have not shed a tear, or experienced an agonizing pang."

To the same : — " When I wrote you last, I was under the influence of *absolute insensibility*. I had not come to my senses. And now that consciousness returns, and I read again your letter, I cannot be happy, until I have expressed to you more freely, how deep a sense I have of the kindness of your heart, in endeavoring to defend me from calumny and abuse, when it was not in my power to defend myself. While this heart is susceptible of emotion, I shall not cease to love you for this, no less than for those virtues I always believed, and now know you to possess."

To another friend she says: "In reference to what I wrote you last, it was *too hard*; it implied *too much*, especially as I suspect I was mistaken in the supposed fact which dictated the remark. I mean in reference to the sentiment commencing with '*I know.*' I beg you to burn the letter, and to blot the remark from your memory. The imagination dictates pictures, as well as magnifies them."

CHAPTER XVIII.

MISS HAZELTINE ENTERS WITH INCREASED VIGOR INTO THE INTERESTS OF HER SCHOOL — VISIT TO NEW HAVEN — LETTERS.

TENDERNESS and affection were now a source of nothing, to Miss Hazeltine, but bitterness and grief. The whole current of her feelings was changed. The absorbing subject of thought was, now, in an important sense, prohibited. To save herself from wretchedness, she applied, with increased vigor, to study. She raised the standard of scholarship, and was constantly devising plans for the advancement of the seminary. The seminary building must be enlarged, and there must be a stately edifice for a boarding establishment. Her correspondence, at this date, exhibits her plans, her joy and hope connected with them, strangely commingling with the bitterness of past remembrances. Her course from this time, in one view, seems enigmatical; yet, when regarded philosophically, perfectly natural. She longed to make the world and herself believe that all was well, and to secure this object, she constantly reiterated the sentiment. Yet all was not well. She feared that the public felt it. This made her feelingly alive to even a look, which implicated her character.

There seemed now, two individual existences combined in her nature. One led to the consideration of everything which was great and glorious. The other to all that was tender and soul-stirring. When the former held the supremacy, she seemed the perfection of happiness. The future was lighted up with rainbow hues. All was joy, all uninterrupted success. When the other principle held the rein, the scene was changed. Then this seemed a dark and gloomy world, everything was adverse.

At the close of the fall term, 1835, she went to pass the winter at New Haven. She felt the need of society and general reading, and resolved to give up the advanced class she had retained during the winter the three years previous, and avail herself of the best society and the best libraries.

She writes to Professor F., dated September 25 : — " I think of passing the winter with a wealthy English lady, in New Haven, for the sake of the advantages of polite society. The family converse with ease in French, and are accustomed to all the refinements of fashionable life ; one of the ladies is the widow of a very excellent minister, lately deceased ; an excellent woman. I have thought of calling and spending a few days with you at Providence, as I go on, should you be there, and could you obtain board for me. I should like to see your premises, school, Providence, and some of its society, and most of all, yourself and family."

After her arrival in New Haven, she thus writes to Mrs. Purkitt : " How much you would be pleased to spend a day or two with me, just to see how prettily and how pleasantly I am living. Everything so nice, and even elegant, and so much pains taken to oblige. Our Yankee friends are exceedingly kind in their way, so sincere and frank ; but there is something in the hospitality of foreigners, certainly of the English, French and Spanish, which is unknown with us.

"This is a very pretty place, Rebecca, though much less so at this season than in summer, as its abundant and beautiful foliage is, perhaps I may say, its principal ornament. There are many very respectable, though few *superb* edifices, the buildings being mostly of wood, painted white. There are nine buildings appropriated to the use of the college ; they have, however, rather a spiritless appearance, being somewhat defaced, with very sunken entrances.

"I have visited the lecture halls of the college, the cabinet of minerals, and the gallery of paintings, am highly pleased with all, especially with the cabinet. This collection is exceedingly splendid. The hall is perhaps thirty by sixty feet, completely filled with cases of the most various and richest specimens on all sides, and on the floor. This gallery too contains many very interesting pictures by Trumbull, aid-de-camp of Washington. Of course, our great hero occupies the foreground of almost every military piece. There are also several touching representations from the New Testament history, especially the representation of our blessed Saviour, sinking beneath the cross, and a tender female supporting his head, and wiping the sweat from his brow. I am occupied chiefly with reading — have not felt able yet to prepare anything for the treasury; have plenty of matter as soon as I can put it into a suitable garb. I am sorry that I find myself very much out of tune for writing; the muses have quite left me; I pray it may not be forever, otherwise I am forsaken indeed. So soon as I *can* do it possibly, I will fulfil all my promises to your husband, but he must be patient.

" I have obtained an introduction to several of the most fashionable families with whom Mrs. R. is familiar, and also with some of the professors and their families. I am truly pleased with them, thus far, making allowance for a little too much of fashionable insignificance among the one class, and of cautious reserve among the other.

" I was never more uniformly cheerful, for which I desire to be thankful. I am truly an astonishment to myself; careless and simple as a child; cheerfulness without and peace within. O, how blessed the truth, that ' there is a balm for those that weep,' that the ' healing leaves ' descend even upon terrestrial ground. I hope I shall never forget the great goodness of my Heavenly Father, in not suffering me to be *quite*, and *for ever*, overwhelmed by the billows of adversity."

In a letter to Miss L. A. Griggs, dated New Haven, Feb. 12, 1836 : — " I have had quite a good time in making up the report, thus far ; hope it will please you, but cannot tell how it will meet the approbation of friends generally, having had the privilege of consulting not one of the other officers ; so that merit or blame must come all upon me. I hope you are enjoying much, *very much*; trust you are. Time was, when I knew the exquisite pleasures you now know — but it is all well. My heart is free from care and sorrow; not *one single* cause disturbs my peace. I feel like nature's child. Every want is satisfied, every wish anticipated, so far as I can ever expect it will be, while here below. I know neither the joys nor the sorrows of life, but a queer sort of passive pleasure, indefinable to yourself, I dare say, and often prompting a smile upon my own square cheek. Forgive me, if I speak as a fool. I suppose you would like to know what is occurring of interest here. I can only say that I am extending my acquaintance, very much to my interest; for although there are few things in common between us *New Hampshire Baptists* and *New Haven Congregationalists*, yet I am reading a new chapter in the volume of human character, or, at least, a chapter possessing *something* of *novelty*. It is not well, I think, to have our notions of men and manners too much circumscribed; we are probably not aware how very limited our own views are, while confined to our little sphere, and that not exactly the centre of the world.

Since I wrote last, we have been honored with calls from the city mayor, accompanied by the Chesterfield of the city, an *honorable*, whose name I will not mention, and from three of the professors; from Mrs. Dwight, lady of the former minister of Park street, Boston, and several other ladies of distinction. Their society is *improving*, although it affords not that exalted pleasure to a stranger, which I should derive from an hour's sweet society of my own dear

Lucy Ann, or any other kindred spirit. Would you believe me, that Miss Sleeper has not written me, except a few hasty lines, with two or three others, in one letter, since I came here? Who could have thought it? Dear Sis! is friendship taking her flight to the land of the blest? — that only plant of paradise, which we fondly hoped had survived the fall, is it a cheating phantom? I will cherish no such belief; either my dear Lucy Ann and Sis Sarah have written to me, or there has been a good reason why they have not done so."

She writes to Mr. Purkitt, Feb. 18 : — " I wrote you some time since, but you have either not received my letter, it seems, or have not had leisure (for surely there could have been no want of inclination) to answer it. Your papers come very regularly, for which I am truly grateful. I am getting along quite well in all matters of consequence, I believe; am passing the time very much to my mind; see just so much company as I choose, and of the best class; have plenty of books to read, pleasant companions, &c. I should be very glad, however, now and then to drop in upon some friends of olden times. O, there are *none* like *these!* Like everything most precious, years but perfect them. They are the bright stars in the shaded hemisphere of life. Such friends you enjoy.

" Pray what is the subject of conversation among you — the exciting Indian and French war? These are times of interest; there is no want of topics of debate. I hear nothing of controversy, however; we happen to be a very quiet family, much inclined to ' leave war and arms to men, to whose province they belong,' as said Turners to Alecto. Indeed, for a week or two, I have kept at home, pretty close, making up that strange kind of compound which you will see in our report. By-the-by, dear sir, can you confer on me a very, *very*, special favor? Have you leisure, have you patience? That you will feel an *interest*, I am quite sure, were it only on my account. Well, then, what? I will tell you: This wonderful report is to be published in Boston, for two reasons; one, because I have a great horror of having anything to do with the *men*, (and you know that printers are men,) the other, that I have greater confidence in my friend, Mr. Ramsey, in relation to matters of type, and all the little matters of punctuation, capitalizing, regulating distances, &c., than in myself. I have entrusted the thing entirely to Perley; but, you recollect, it was with the understanding that I should see the proofs. So you will just consult with him, if you please, as I should do. I feel particularly anxious that the thing should be done up in good style, because it is my concern so absolutely; not having Professor Smith or any of the honorable board, at my elbow.

" What is Rebecca doing? It is coming spring directly; indeed I am quite frightened; where will my winter, so long doated upon, have fled? Like a passing shadow of a cloud upon the waving corn, I am sure. O, how do these visions of bright scenes flit over my mind! I mean, scenes, when I looked with an inward, untroubled, hoping heart, upon the rural landscapes of my own happy home; when my

15*

dear mother imparted life and loveliness to the dwelling, to which I looked down from the verdant slopes of my native hills? But she sleeps in death, and knows not the desolations of heart which her absence causes; she knows not the sorrows of her unhappy child. These are the shades, which sometimes sweep the soul, when, as in the present case, some mental allusion touches its living chords.

"I am to spend this evening at Professor Olmsted's; anticipate much pleasure. You would like this man; and his wife is very amiable too. I think I could easily become quite attached here, if my business made it my home. My affections, however, are all *my own*; I am aloof from all the world. Not an object beneath the concave heavens, on which I doat. My friends I love, but it is with a sublimity of feeling, rather than that strong instinctive attachment which simple childhood knew. I love them for their virtues, not because nature bids me. I love them as dearest treasures, soon to be left behind. But I seem resolutely bent, by some strange fatality, to fall upon the sentimental to-day. You must be sure and let Rebecca see this, lest she should think I am making an attempt to steal your heart. Please give my best regards to Br. Hadley's family; tell them I have every comfort I can ask, and hope they are able to . keep themselves warm and cheerful, I expect this will pass for a cold winter, will it not? We have geat quantities of snow here. Tell Rebecca, she is one of the chaste nymphs, which my imagination loves to cherish, as my airy attendants through these void regions of space. I have really a band of sweet sisters, among whom I delight to dance. *Bright airy forms.* Now, don't you think I shall become a poet? This would make amends for all. Poor ' Young,' however, I am afraid, would be my model, and then, in return for all the favors of my friends, I should only repay them with sighs and tears. This would not be kind, do you think it would? So I think I will become a better prose writer first ; as the sage, calculating Yankees say, ' better learn all the English branches first, and then, if you like, study Latin.' "

Young was, at this time, a favorite author with her. Notwithstanding her endeavors to be, and to appear, both in her epistolary correspondence and personal intercourse, " as happy as a child," having " not a single cause of sorrow," yet it could not be disguised that she inwardly, and too deeply, sympathized in the sad, melancholy strains of the " Night Thoughts." The following lines, strongly marked by her pencil, while reading it about this time, reflect some light upon the real tone of her feelings : —

> " And from an eye
> Of tenderness let heavenly pity fall
> On me, more justly numbered with the dead."

> " All, all on earth is shadow ; all beyond
> Is substancé ; the reverso is Folly's creed."

> " The spider's most attenuated thread
> Is cord, is cable, to man's tender tie
> On earthly bliss."

> " Each moment has its sickle, emulous
> Of time's enormous scythe.
> Each moment plays
> His little weapon in a narrower sphere

Of sweet domestic comfort, and cuts down
The fairest bloom of sublunary bliss.
Bliss! sublunary bliss!—proud words and vain!
I clasp'd the phantom, and I found it air.
Oh, had I weighed it ere my fond embrace!
What darts of agony had missed my heart."

" How distant oft the thing we doat on most,
From that for which we dote, felicity!"

CHAPTER XIX.

CORRESPONDENCE OF 1836-7.

Miss Hazeltine's correspondence during the year 1836 is full of schemes. After her return from New Haven, she writes to Miss Griggs, who had then become a teacher at Townsend, dated May 26: "Alas! for thee, my sister, where art thou? O how much I have enjoyed, in sympathy with your joy, since your school commenced! This, you may be sure, has been purely disinterested pleasure. You are removed from my side, and from my sight too, but not from my remembrance or affection. Blessings upon thee, sister. May thy happy heart never know sorrow.

"Your successor, Miss Colby, does admirably. Quite a rival to yourself, we think, in stealing hearts. We miss you, however, painfully, in our morning exercises, and in our meetings. But the thought that perhaps you are acting with increased effect, where you are, hushes our rising sighs.

"We hardly know our prospects for the future, yet, we Yankees are very deliberate, a calculating people. It is perfectly right, you know, to count the cost before beginning to build. Our friends seem very sin-

cere ánd true, and manifest an excellent spirit. We
had quite an unexpected addition of black coats to
our school one morning ; some seven or eight, I believe. So I gave them a lesson in theology, ('I
mean biblical theology,') of course, as I thought this
might be of more *immediate use* to them than the languages.

"Our own family is just the best that ever was.
Miss Field occupies her old room ; but she is profoundly studious, and has a room-mate whom I cannot commend in too strong terms. An excellent
Christian, and a lovely girl. Everything is of course
quiet there. Then there is Miss Hill, with a room-
mate quite like herself; then Mary Raymond in your
room, with her sister Nancy. Miss Colby and Miss
Elizabeth Freeman, in the front room opposite to
ours ; and Sis Sarah and I constitute the comple-
ment."

She writes to the same, May 31 : — "I am enjoying
good spirits, excellent classes, a pleasant home and
kind associates. I do not feel as much religious enjoyment as I desire. I have too much to do. We
have been obliged to admit more classes than usual
this term, so that I am obliged to hear nine classes
myself daily. This is too hard, Lucy Ann ; it makes
me very much fatigued often, and gives me no time
to visit, and too little for meditation and prayer. I
shall try to get off some of my burden soon ; I must
do so for the sake of our religious interests. Our
Berian Society is more interesting than heretofore.
Instead of facts merely, we have each one present
some reflection of her own, in connection, if she

chooses, with some fact or sentiment of another.
The young ladies are prompt, when called upon for
any duty ; but we do not feel sufficiently anxious for
sinners. O, how little are we influenced by those
things which are spiritual and eternal! Dear sister,
let us pray for each other, that great grace may be
given us, that we may form our pupils for happiness
and heaven. You have many friends who love you
and pray for you ; so perhaps I am arrogant enough
to hope you will often think of me, and that with interest ; indeed, I will not claim too much ; *I* shall
not cease to remember *you* with affection. I long to
hear more particularly of your welfare and prosperity. We thought you were feeling the chastening
influence of care and responsibility a little. I often
think of an expressive line of Mrs. Hemans, ' That
early faded through fond care for him.' Maternal
cares are not yours and mine, but ours, perhaps, are
scarcely less wearing. This is of but little consequence, however, so long as we feel that our cause
is a good one."

She writes to Mr. Ramsey, her nephew, July 7 : —
" You have thrown me into such a dilemma, that I
know not how to extricate myself ; for in either case
I see that I am to be convicted of fault. As it is my
motto, however, that ' honesty is the best policy,' my
course, I perceive, is very direct, and I must plainly
tell you, that nothing but stern necessity has prevented me from writing to you. I did very wrong in
the spring to assume so much labor ; but I felt well,
and it seemed unavoidable. I am still in good health,
but so much hurried, as to render my situation rather

uncomfortable. This is one of my greatest troubles. And since you wish me to tell you freely all the sources of my sorrows and of my joys, I will avail myself of the privilege very gratefully. Well then, I often think of my poor, disconsolate father, daily becoming more feeble, and clinging to me with a confidence and tenacity to which I do not feel adequate to respond. I cannot listen to a tale of sorrow from a friend, without feeling too deeply. I have sometimes felt afraid that I shall not always enjoy as much health and vigor as I have done, and that I shall not be able to render myself agreeable and serviceable to society. And sometimes I fear that my religious hopes are not well based. I do not doubt the efficacy of the gospel system to procure the eternal and complete happiness of all who embrace it; but I fear I have received it in intellectual apprehension, rather than with the whole soul. These, together with occasional vexations arising from the care of so many whose principles of action are not established, and whose intellectual character is but sketched, make up the sum of my miseries. I still have many pleasures. I think I have to some degree the confidence of my pupils, and the satisfaction to hope I am contributing something to their future well-being. Besides, I am greatly indebted to my Heavenly Father for the profusion of the common blessings of life. I do not know want, of any description, and have much real comfort. How thankful an individual thus circumstanced ought to be!"

In a letter to Miss Griggs, dated July 14, she says, "I have had too much to do this summer, altogether;

doubt whether I shall be able to do much at examination. I fear for my classes, particularly; it is impossible to treat a dozen as we could do half that number.

"You have very much to do, Sis; if I mistake not seven or eight classes in the long days. I must tell you as many have told me, when I smiled at their well-*meant* simplicity, 'You must be careful of your health.' I am resolved, if I teach another term, never to assume as much as I have done this, let the consequences be what they may. I am glad you are situated so pleasantly; can fully sympathize with you in your anxieties and in your pleasures. Responsibility is not the worst of evils; indeed, a degree of it is a pleasure. I hope your heart will be rejoiced to see the conversion of your pupils. May the Lord bless you abundantly.

"I hope Mr. and Mrs. Purkitt will spend the vacation with me. This will contribute greatly to my pleasure, as you can easily conceive. I am anticipating some good rides with them; do not know but I shall be disappointed, however. I must not calculate upon too much. How often are our brightest visions beclouded! I have learned to view this world as it is, I think, and not to hope more from it than it is capable of yielding. O, may I but be fitted for heaven! how blessed it will be to depart thither! I think I enjoy more peaceful confidence in God, this season, than is usual for me. I can now enjoy prayer. You know what I have sometimes said to you upon this subject; but it is not so now. God is my only portion, and I hope I do love him. What

16

can I want more? I do not think other blessings so indispensable, as I have sometimes done. God can make us happy in any condition in which we are placed by his providence. I place no less value upon earthly friends, than I have done at any time; and yet, I do not feel that one must necessarily be *so miserable* without a FRIEND. I have great reason to bless God for the support he has afforded me; it is possible for human nature to sustain very much and yet survive."

She writes to the same, September 17 : — " My vacation I found very pleasant and refreshing, after a toilsome term. My friends came as I anticipated, and we journeyed to the White Mountains again. You will hardly think this was judicious for me; but I was very desirous of doing so, and enjoyed it very much. It was refreshing, Lucy Ann; can you conceive it? To behold the same objects, listen to the same echo, sit in the same chamber? I felt sad, but time had so tempered my feelings, as to render the scene a luxury. O, I do love those solitudes, those simple wilds of nature; there is something so sacred in them — to me, doubly so. It was there I enjoyed my last visit with my friend. Professors Smith and Pearce passed the day in which our gentlemen ascended the mountain, with myself and Mrs. Purkitt in the celebrated Notch. Morse and White were there, but left in the morning. We returned by way of Littleton, a fine little village, and Haverhill. Mrs. P. made me a dear good visit. O, how I love congenial souls! she is one, truly.

" We are now two weeks advanced upon our second

term; have enough to do, but have managed to reduce our labor to something a little more approxi-
mating to what is reasonable, than last term. My
health is perfectly good again. I am very thankful,
for I was really afraid, last term, that I should lose
my voice. It was speaking too much, I am now
quite certain. Our societies are prosperous, and feel
very much interested in the studies, especially those
which are biblical. We hope one young lady has
found peace in believing within a few days. Our
examination was not satisfactory to me; that is, not
very much so, but I am not so sensitive as to worry
much about it. It passed off better than I had reason to expect, considering the almost absolute pros-
tration of health, both of myself and Miss Sleeper,
not to say Misses Barker and Colby. But these
things have somewhat less interest for me than they
once had; that is, they have not such a hold upon
my imagination. I hope you will not allow yourself
to be excited by such things; the effect is exceedingly deleterious to the constitution."

She writes to her nephew, Oct. 18: — "I am enjoying myself much the present term; have not had so
good health and spirits for many years. My journey
in August did me incalculable good. I am full of
schemes for the future, in respect to usefulness, not
particularly to fame. I am not yet decided, where
to spend the winter; shall employ it somewhere in
close study. ~

"I am sorry for the disappointments of your firm,
in which you must of course participate. But this
is the common lot, Pearley. It is good for a man to

bear the yoke in his youth. Do not be discouraged. I will be your friend, ‘if this is any consolation.’ Only have care of your health. This is a world, and a period of enterprise, and there are more places and means than one, of getting a fortune. You must keep your eye open to good chances of enterprise, and when you are able, make some profitable investment, and so on. We will not be poor, kind providence blessing us. I hope, my dear friend, that you will rightly interpret all the dealings of a kind, Heavenly Father in respect to yourself; you may scarcely indulge the thought that he has a care for you; but I regard the question in a very different light. Nothing happens by chance, Pearley; kindness is couched in every seeming frown. The more I study God's scheme of government, as administered in the present world, with reference to a future, the more am I lost in admiration. What we see not now, we shall see hereafter, and it will appear, I doubt not, unspeakably to God's praise. You will excuse me for giving my topic a serious turn; you gave me leave, I think once, to write you on serious subjects, if I chose; and you will excuse me, if I manifest a peculiar anxiety that, before your habits become so settled as to be inflexible, your character be moulded by the principles of the gospel. Do not let the hope of gain, on the one hand, nor the vexation of disappointment, on the other, so engross your feelings, as to prevent a calm, deliberate consideration of the subject of religion. This period of toil and strife, of hopes and disappointments, will soon close upon us forever; then, whose will these things be, for which we have toiled. How happy will it be for us, if we are found, at that day, to have laid up our treasure in heaven."

In a letter to Miss Patterson, dated Oct. 17, she says, " I have great and glorious schemes in my mind. Now you smile, as well you may, at my vanity and self-conceit, in the notion of accomplishing anything illustrious myself. But it matters not, you know, so long as I think so ; I am just as much interested, and just as happy in the anticipation, as if it were reasonable. You must know, as I suppose you do already, that we are making preparations for a large boarding-house for our department, and for such alterations and additions with respect to our chapel and recitation building, as our circumstances require. I am engaged, of course, in making plans, preparing drafts, &c. In this work, I beg leave to solicit your co-operation. Will you do me the special favor to give me a small sketch of the plan of Mrs. Willard's buildings. Will you tell me what you regard as the leading excellences of her system, and the most valuable traits in her character ? How does the fashionable cast of her school affect the state of religion in the heart ? How far would you recommend an attention to style and fashion in the policy of a school ?

" Now, my dear Mary, in order to gratify me with remarks upon all these subjects, you will need to write me a letter closer than usual, I am aware, and perhaps I am unreasonable in tasking you so severely ; and yet I have one more thing to request, that is, the literary article which I was to have had last year. If you can forward it within four weeks, so as to have it presented to the association before the close of the session, so much the more acceptable; if not, let me have it as soon after as may be. Do not fail in this particular; I have made my arrangements for the report with reference to this article, and cannot be disappointed. I shall insert the article entire, so you will have regard to the limits accordingly. Do not be so brief as not to do justice to your theme; with this caution, condensation is a virtue, as you know."

To Miss Griggs. Nov. 22 : — "I did not mean, last summer term, ever to be so much engaged in school duties again; but although I was able in the fall to manage so as to render my task more tolerable, I found no more leisure than before. Be assured, my affection for you was never stronger or more lively than at present. The fact, that you have interests in some respects independent of mine, produces not the slightest alienation of feeling in my bosom. Indeed, I consider our interests the same. In my view of the subject, we are strictly co-workers. The arrangements of God's Providence requires that his laborers should occupy different stations, in point of locality; but the scheme is *one*, the great design *one*. I despise that narrow spirit which cannot rejoice in the prosperity of one of kindred calling. O, my sister, how unworthy the blessed Gospel, how unworthy of everything exalted in human character is such a spirit! May Heaven preserve me from it!

"You will be curious to know why I am here, with nothing to do. I will tell you. You know I am so much engaged in the immediate duties of instruction during the term-time, as to afford me little leisure for general reading. Besides our present scheme, as

sketched in the catalogue, will require much reviewing and much reading, in order to perfect it. I am
to examine text books, and to determine many matters of detail. You smile, and ask me if I expect
such a scheme to go into operation at *New Hampton?*
I answer, if not *here,* I think it may somewhere else.
My time and thoughts will not be lost, I hope. Sanguine expectations are entertained, however, of its
being effected here! I am not over solicitous about
it, am but *one,* and can find a place sufficiently large
for *me,* almost anywhere."

In the summer following, (1837), everything connected with the seminary bespoke advancement.
The seminary building had been enlarged to twice its
original size. The assembly room, drawing hall, and
the several halls for recitation were now ample and
convenient. The plan for a new boarding edifice
had been projected, several of the workmen engaged,
and the work commenced. This building was designed to accommodate a hundred pupils. It seemed
the consummation of hope. Everything around had
begun to wear a different aspect. Improvement had
advanced as the exigencies of the times demanded.
Pleasant dwelling houses, and buildings for merchants
and mechanics, were being raised every day. The
surrounding landscape was increasing with interest,
and the imagination pictured this " Switzerland of
America," the most pleasant residence in the country.
It was believed that pleasant walks and shady classic
groves would soon grace every side — that it must
become the abode of the muses, the permanent dwel-
ling-place of science and literature.

Through the summer, prosperity crowned every effort. At the public examination, all the friends were present. Its principal patrons seemed fired with the spirit of benevolence and hope. Every one felt that nought could impede the progress of the school, now in so prosperous a state. But the hopes were now too sanguine to be of long continuance. A few months after this period, the institution was doomed to feel misfortune in the death of its first, and one of its principal patrons. J. K. Simpson, who had watched the interests of the institution and seminary from their commencement, with all the anxiety of a father, was not permitted to witness the consummation of his hopes in the erection of the boarding edifice. He died suddenly, December, 1837, after only a few days illness. This, at first, seemed a death-blow to hope. The idea of erecting a building upon the generous plan already projected, now became perfectly chimerical. It was therefore abandoned. Yet hope did not fail. From the first the friends of the institution had put their chief confidence in divine power, and they felt that, perhaps, this sudden affliction was but to make them realize the source of all their blessings and prosperity.

Miss H. says of this year, in a letter to the honorary members of the association connected with the seminary : — "The past year has presented a mingled scene of sad and joyous changes, and such may we expect in future. How delightful to feel that we are the care of Providence ; that we are under the administration of an infinitely wise and benevolent Being ! In the midst of affliction we may kiss the rod, and commit ourselves with a trusting confidence to a faithful Creator.

" Dear sisters, your sensibility has doubtless perceived a significancy in these allusions; your sympathies we have already shared; we thank you for them. There are so many tender chords in the human heart, that it is scarcely safe to touch them by adverting to an event which has borne so directly upon our dearest interests; we allude to the death of our friend and patron, J. K. Simpson. Of our loss, as individuals, we forbear to speak; as a seminary, it would seem irreparable. But it is not so. In the language of another, which was a timely cordial to our spirits, ' though the departed be no longer our *living* patron, our *chief patron lives.*' This is our consolation, and enables us to triumph over adversity.

" But we should be very ungrateful, were we to dwell alone upon the afflictive dispensations of our Heavenly Father. In no year have we experienced more signal mercies. We have not forgotten the little handful of precious grain we were allowed to gather, in the earlier harvest, as the fruit of the incorruptible seed of divine truth scattered in our midst; nor the more signal displays of the omnipotent power of the gospel, recently experienced among our brethren. With Zion all around, we are permitted to lift our hearts with rejoicing, for the ' voice of the turtle is heard in our land.'

"In other respects, too, our interests have prospered, both abroad and at home. We have noticed no death among our numbers during the past year; and very few have suffered from severe illness. So far as our knowledge has extended, there has occurred no instance of failure or disgrace among those who have gone forth under our auspices. In our extracts from the many letters of our correspondents, we have been entirely impartial; we have suppressed nothing which might have exposed truths prejudicial to our interests, but have reported the evil with the good; and yet we cannot forbear felicitating ourselves, and, we hope, rendering thanks to God for the result.

" At home, our friends are endeavoring to meet, as far as possible, the exigencies of our present condition, arising from providential delays in reference to our contemplated edifice for boarding. Our chapel-hall and recitation rooms are already ample, our library increasing, and our board of teachers full. We design to organize the school according to the accompanying schedule, as nearly as practicable, and hope to realize, what our fond wishes have long aspired to, the satisfaction of graduating honorably, from year to year, a class whom we may not fear to submit to the trying test of action on the stage of human life.

" Thus much for ourselves. To those who are in remote or foreign lands, we tender our warmest sympathies. We love to accompany them, in heart, in their labors of compassion and love, and rejoice to know that their hands are not weak, nor their hearts faint. We pledge them our prayers, rendered more fervent, we trust, by their late communications, and our efforts, so far as God shall give us ability. May we, who are at home, emulate our sisters in the ' far west,' and those in the east, the *far east*,* in the work of holy benevolence, and we shall share their crown.

> " In much affection, yours,
> > " M. HAZELTINE, *Cor. Sec.*"

The schedule, to which she refers, presented the regular course of studies for each year to be pursued in the seminary. The scholars, in the spring of 1839, were, according to attainment, classed in the several years. We now graduate a class yearly, with an amount of discipline rarely attained previous to submitting to the trying " test of action on the stage of human life."

* See Mrs. Wade's Address to Christian Females in New York and Brooklyn.

CHAPTER XX.

To her Father.

I HAVE been somewhat troubled since I wrote, lest you should take as unkind some of my last remarks. But I knew you were accustomed to exercise much forbearance towards me, and so I was perhaps too bold. If so, I hope you will forgive me. I am sure I did not intend to be disrespectful, and was prompted solely by the motives which I expressed ; the good of the cause of Christ as affected by your last testimony. I still think the sentiments of an aged Christian who has been known and distinguished as a friend to religion, have an important influence on the surviving generation, and consequently have felt very anxious that you might exhibit, to the last, the power of the religion of Jesus, to destroy every unholy propensity under the most unfavorable circumstance. I pray that the grace of God may enable you thus to do. I hope you are in the enjoyment of every good, and doubt not you have a share of trials, which are not the least of our mercies. Without them, how could our souls receive that exercise and discipline necessary to fit them for glory ? I think the sentiments of the apostle, who says, " they shall work for us a far more exceeding and eternal weight of glory," very forcible and just.   Let us not, therefore, be anxious to avoid afflictions, but to have them sanctified to us.   Let us bear hardness as good soldiers, and endure trials with christian fortitude. God knows best what afflictions we need ; then let us kiss the rod and the hand of him that hath appointed it.   Doubtless the remaining corruptions of our hearts will appear, while we are under trials ; and this our heavenly Father intends, that we may not flatter ourselves that we are holy, but that we may discover our need of daily forgiveness, and of the sanctifying influences of the Holy Spirit.   Let us then count it all joy, when we fall into divine temptations, looking to our Deliverer to make for us a way of escape.

May the peace of God which passeth all understanding, abide both with you and me, and the Holy Spirit guide us into all truth.   Love to my dear brothers and sisters.

Your affectionate daughter,

MARTHA.

To her Brother J.

I wish I could sit down and converse with you this evening, and offer you something comforting.   I would present you with some of the views which gladden my own mind and render me cheerful and happy, amidst the adversities incident to our present condition.   I regard all our unhappiness as arising, either directly or indirectly, from a want of conformity to the will of God, and believe that our happiness is

promoted and secured, in proportion as our disposi-
tions are made to harmonize with the divine will.
Even the ills which the irrevocable sentence of Jehovah upon our fallen race has made inseparable from
our present condition, are virtually removed, when
our minds are brought to acquiesce cheerfully in the
righteousness of the sentence, and to see its connexion
with his own most glorious perfection. The first
proposition is founded, I think, upon the soundest
philosophy, and the latter, is a point of common
observation. If your mind, dear brother, could be
brought to a complete understanding of the gospel
plan of salvation, and your feelings could be turned
into a current harmonizing with the truths therein
displayed, I am sure there would be no need of your
ever having any more bitterness of spirit, either in
this world or in the world to come. Only receive
the pardon of your past sins through Jesus Christ,
which is freely tendered you, if you will receive it in
this way, and turn the affections of your heart to
holiness, or conformity to the will of God, and the
work is done. When you were in all the pride of
your strength, you could not find it in your heart to
receive the humiliating doctrines of Christ; but now,
that God has subdued your spirit by sickness, he has
peculiarly disposed you to submit to him. I hope
you will regard this kind, but afflictive providence,
as coming from the hands of that great and good
Being, who has no pleasure in the death of the sinner, but rather that he turn and live. You never
will be happy, unless you can degrade your mind so
much as to be satisfied with the enjoyments of birds

and butterflies, until you possess religion. *It is not among the possibilities of our nature.* You have only to will it, and it is done. All the difficulty is in our own obstinacy. You have all the freedom of your will in relation to holiness, as you have in relation to that which is opposed to holiness. Only exercise the freedom in choosing to act, and think, and feel in harmony with God, and all is well. You possess, in this way, a preparation of heart to enjoy the bliss of heaven, and by faith in Jesus Christ, you shall possess a title to this blessedness. Now, while true happiness is so completely within your reach, is it worth while to drag out your life in wretchedness? I do not think so, and am persuaded that you do not. It is not necessary then, for me to use any persuasion with you, though I might use many arguments drawn from the compassion of God for wretched sinners; but I forbear. I hope you will inform me that you have, after so long a time, come to the enjoyment of a hope, which shall be as an anchor to your soul cast within the vail whither Jesus our forerunner hath for us entered. With the most earnest wishes for your happiness, I subscribe myself your affectionate sister,

MARTHA.

To a Friend teaching in the Sabbath School.

What variety have you this winter to keep the current of life in motion? Does your sabbath school flourish? Are any of your pupils becoming pious? Do you enjoy freedom and comfort in teaching them the principles of our holy religion? Are you becoming better and better acquainted with those sacred truths yourself, and are they exerting a sanctifying influence upon your life? The sermon to-day was from this text: "If ye sow unto the spirit, ye shall of the spirit reap life everlasting." The minister endeavored to prove that the reward of the Christian in a future world, although by no means a reward of debt, but of mere grace, will be in exact proportion to our faithfulness, self-denial, and persevering christian effort while on earth. And is it not so? I believe it is according to the word of God. Have we thought enough of this? O, my dear, let us shake off our indolent habits, as well as those which are more flagrant. So shall we imitate him who went about doing good. So shall we glorify him, by bearing much fruit. So shall we be his disciples. Are not these considerations enough to stimulate us to be faithful?

I am reading Hannah More's Practical Piety. If you have never read it I think you will find it very profitable. She observes that the Christian will never be idle, while there is distress to relieve in another, or a corruption to be cured in his own heart. We have employments assigned us for every condition in life. When we are alone we have our thoughts to watch; in the family, our tempers; in company, our tongues. "It is a great and difficult thing, Rebecca, to keep our hearts faithfully;" to bring every thought into subjection to Christ; and yet this is unquestionably our duty. O, let us not be remiss. Our season of warfare will be *very short*, and our rest, *very long*. Will you write me particularly the exercises of your mind, and something of your progress in religion?

What do our good Boston folks think of **Mr.**
Judson's letter? Does it share the same fate as **Mrs.**
Wade's? For my own part, I do feel rather scrupu-
lous in expending so much for dress, when we might
appear quite as well with half the expense. The
fact is, we ought to hear to reason about this thing,
and not so much to fashion. Do you not think so?
Rebecca, have we not courage enough to be singular,
if the cause of Christ requires it? If not, should we
ever have submitted to the ordinance of baptism,
unless it had been fashionable? I really want some
of your best, and most candid thoughts on this subject. I know it is somewhat difficult to determine on
the details of dress; but after all, ought the admission
of this to put a stay to the argument, as it has been
wont to do? We wish to do what will please our
heavenly Father, even if it entails reproach and persecution, otherwise, we are unworthy to be called his
disciples. We ought, then, at least to give the subject a candid examination.

To Miss Mitchell.

I am really thankful to know that you have obtained strength enough to profess Christ publicly.
I hope you enjoy more comfort now, though I
presume you may still be fearful, at times, that
you have gone too far. I hope you have not. I
think there is much more probability that you
have not gone far enough. If you are at any
time afraid, that you have presumed too much, in
daring to be baptized and professing to be a Christian, you must think that you will strive to make

17*

your profession good by becoming, immediately, what you profess to be, if you are not so now. In this way, you will not "give place to the devil." "But I hope better things of you, though I thus write. I hope you do not see through a glass so darkly, but enjoy the light of life; that a new song is put into your mouth, even praise to God; that you have the oil of joy, for mourning; that you have gone forth weeping, bearing precious seed; and that you are now enjoying the sheaves. Well then, rejoice ever more, pray without ceasing, and in everything give thanks, for this is the will of God concerning us."

To a Nephew.

I am very glad that you succeed so well in your business, that you possess such an aptitude to acquire what is useful, and that you have been thus far assisted in obtaining the object of your wishes, a knowledge of your art. I trust you will not now be abandoned. I am sure you will not, if you put your trust in Him, whose is the silver and the gold, and in whose hands are the hearts of all men. This has been my hope for you, and is so still. I think you will not launch out upon an untried ocean, in a frail bark, without a pilot. You know that "all flesh is grass," and "cursed is he that putteth his trust in man, or maketh flesh his arm;" but the care of the Lord is omnipotent, and "blessed is every one that trusteth in Him." I cannot tell you what an unspeakable relief it is to me to repair to the Omnipotent God, when in perplexity. I have had the trial of it within a few months. I was in doubt what course to pursue in future, and saw nothing but difficulty, let me do what I would. These objects of terror have now vanished. God has led me hitherto, and I have felt to trust him for the future. I remember, Perley, on the day that I was seventeen, I endeavored to surrender myself into the hands of God, and to beseech him that he would be my guardian through life; and O, I bless the day, and have, on several birth-days since, renewed my self-dedication and my request. How many evils I have thus escaped, and how many blessings I have thus enjoyed, it is impossible for me to say. One thing I *can* say, that it is good to trust in God, and that I would not on any account, for worlds, be abandoned to my own inclinations. I hope my dear nephew would not consider it unmanly to acknowledge, and cherish a dependence upon the Great God. Instead of its being a shame, it is our greatest glory. We can aspire after nothing higher than the most entire submission to his will, and the fullest devotion of ourselves and all that appertains to us, to his cause. With him for your friend, you possess all things; you need have no anxiety, for all things shall work together for your good, even adversity shall be a blessing, and amidst the deepest afflictions you shall adopt the language of triumph. I would not urge thus upon you the importance of seeking first the kingdom of God and his righteousness, if I felt less interested for your happiness; and if this letter abounds too much in the serious, impute it to my excess of affectionate solicitude for you. God has given you life, he has endowed you with all the powers, both physical and mental, which you pos-

sess. Your literary acquirements are no less his
gift, than your original faculties, and what more
reasonable, than that these, his benefits, should be
appropriated according to his will. Dear nephew,
you have found yourself a fallen creature, with inclinations opposed to God, although his character is
spotless, and in the highest degree lovely; now, if
you hate him without a cause, whether you were ac-
cessory, or not, to your possessing these propensities
originally, is it not just, is it anything more than just,
is it not your imperious duty, to refuse to cherish such
unjustifiable sentiments, and to become immediately,
heartily, reconciled to God, especially since he has
done so much to make reconciliation to himself possible through the blood of his Son? I beseech you
not to live longer in unbelief, if you have thus lived
hitherto; but I hope you have already received the
Gospel, not as the word of man, but, as it is in truth,
the word of God.

To the same.

I regard the establishment of a stable character, and the formation of virtuous habits, as of infinitely more importance than any other attainment,
however valuable in itself. Study to be always
industrious, economical, and prudent in the most
extensive sense, and you cannot fail to be successful and happy. I should think you had much to
contribute to your enjoyment, and quite an opportunity for improvement. Three hours each day properly applied to reading, cannot fail to produce much
effect upon your mind. It will put you in possession
of many important facts, if devoted to history, or do

much towards the cultivation of your taste, if directed to poetry, and serve to form your style of writing, if employed in studying the classics. Let each of these branches of reading suitably divide your leisure hours. But the exercise, which of all will be of the most importance to you, is *reflection*. The art of thinking is worth your most persevering effort; I mention this particularly, as I think your present course unfavorable to such effort. The discipline which is acquired by the study of the languages and mathematics, you will be likely to want, in a course of miscellaneous reading. Close application to composing is the best substitute for these studies, and for this you have peculiar facilities. I intend to consult Professor F. respecting the best order of reading, and if I can settle upon anything which I think will be of any service to you, I will communicate it with the greatest pleasure.

To Miss Hannah Smith, sister of Mr. Joseph Smith.

I am much pleased to think you are teaching; I think it will afford you an excellent discipline; and hope you are patient and kind to your little charge. O, how responsible are the duties of a teacher! You cannot estimate your influence over the future character of your pupils. I hope your course is decidedly religious. You should always bear in mind, that the ultimate aim of every teacher should be to render his charge virtuous in the highest degree. Mould not the mind alone, but see to it that you form the moral character with the utmost care. O, what is it, my dear, to receive into our charge gems so invaluable as the immortal mind, to be formed and polished by our hands! Let us not trifle with such responsibilities, for they are awfully solemn. And yet, the duties and privileges of a teacher are enviable. Who does not count it an honor to be permitted to engage in some arduous enterprise, especially if it be exalted? And what enterprise more arduous and more exalted than the formation of the human mind? Strive, my dear Hannah, to obtain, in an eminent degree, those qualifications which are requisite to enable you to act well your part in the character which you now sustain, and you will have it in your power greatly to augment the sum of human happiness, while you taste the sweet pleasures of knowing that you are carrying forward in some humble degree, the benevolent designs of your Heavenly Parent. Strive to be useful. Spurn self-indulgence and sloth. Be active in forming plans for benevolent effort, and persevere in carrying them into effect, and may the Lord bless you, and make you a blessing.

To the same.

I am glad that you are still teaching at L.; I think it speaks well for you. It seems that you are steady, that you enjoy your health, and that you acquit yourself well of your duty. All this is as could be wished. It only remains to be ascertained if you are enjoying a peaceful and happy state of mind; if you are in the daily performance of every christian duty. I hope this is the case; if not, something is wrong, and should be obviated. I am not sufficiently acquainted with the present state of your feelings to give you any suitable advice ; you do not need any, because you have ample counsel in the precious Bible, the more sure word of testimony, to which we shall do well to take heed. O, do not let your days run to waste ; so few and so precious as they are ! Strive to live to God, the remainder of your time. If you have not made a public profession of religion, it is surely your immediate duty ; and you are doing wrong every day you neglect it. You cannot pursue a course which shall meet the approbation of God, while you neglect this ordinance. Is not this a good time, now that you are at home? Perhaps this is your intention ; perhaps even before now you have submitted to the solemn rite, and are prepared henceforth to walk in all the commandments and ordinances of the Lord blameless. If so, let me offer you my warmest congratulations.

To the same.

I hope you have become a Christian philosopher ; I should think you might be, at present, in a good school for the attainment of meekness and true gentleness. These, it seems to me, are traits of *female character*, surpassed by no others. I hope you will be especially careful to cherish them, and strive to attain, if possible, a perfect control over your spirit. This is the lesson I am trying to learn. I do not like to see ladies act upon the defensive very much. If I am a " peace man " in nothing else, I believe I am here, in *principle*. I should not value very highly as an encomium, the praise of knowing how to scold, or even of possessing a determination to *stand up for my right.* I admire to see a *woman* bear and forbear. I am dealing in *precepts* now, you understand ; example is *another* thing. You must be able to give me a pattern of these virtues, one of these days, when I shall act in a character especially requiring them. What books do you read? What for intellectual improvement, and what for growth in piety? I have just been reading the Memoir of Boardman. It is a charming volume. I think you cannot read it without sighing to be a missionary. Do you never think of it? I desire very much to know if you are a truly devoted Christian ; if you live in habits of intimate communion with God. I think I desire this very much, and I hope am endeavoring to attain a *habit* of deep piety. O, this is what I think I desire, more than anything else. I do think we may live above the world, so as to partake in no small degree of the pure joys of heaven, every day we live. Of this, Brainard, Pearce, and our late beloved Boardman, are illustrious examples. O, for their piety! If you can obtain Abott's Corner Stone, you will find in some of its early pages, a very interesting description of the youthful character of our dear Redeemer. He was the most lovely and perfect pattern which the annals of history anywhere present us. Let us endeavor to form our characters after this model. I think if we should study the character of our Saviour more *minutely,* it would have an excellent effect upon our piety. We seem too much inclined to deal in *generals* here, as if it were enough to concede, that he was without fault. When we examine his character closely, and meditate upon its traits one by one, we shall find occasion for the most forcible and specific terms, to set it forth. Let us keep our Saviour always before our eyes, till his image is indelibly engraven upon our hearts. Beholding him, we shall be changed into his image. And let us endeavor to render our piety practical. 'Herein is my Father glorified, that ye bear much fruit, so shall ye be my disciples.' Be very watchful, my dear girl, that no proud, unholy thoughts be indulged in your heart; be childlike; let your heart be all submission to the *humbling*, but glorious doctrine of the gospel. Remember Jesus was meek and lowly, and seek above all things, the grace of *humility*. The term implies *much*. Search your own heart carefully, and resolve to bring every thought into submission to Christ. Excuse my earnestness. I ardently desire for you the same good things which I most crave for myself.

CHAPTER XXI.

THE summer of 1838, through Mr. Smith's influence, five young ladies from Rhode Island attended school at New Hampton. Mr. Smith, as an acquaintance of the young ladies, wrote a letter of introduction to Miss Hazeltine. The commencement was "Dear Madam;" the close "very respectfully." During the season, one of these young ladies wished to unite with the church at New Hampton. Miss H. wrote to Mr. Smith, as the lady's pastor, inquiring concerning her qualifications for church membership. In the reply, Mr. Smith referred to his own success in the ministry, his abundant labors, the prevailing sickness in his vicinity, his own exposure to death, and closed by consigning to her the letters he had addressed to her during their correspondence, in case he should be a victim to the epidemic then prevailing, saying he had kept them "for *her sake*." The following was her reply :

"My dear Sir, — As it will be a long time before the young ladies return, by whom I have designed to write you, I embrace an opportunity, which now presents itself, of sending to you, by private hand, in order the sooner to assure you that your last was gratefully received.   Let me thank you for your bequest.   It was the most grateful you could have made me.   But I trust you will yet give them me with your own hand.   I fear, however, exceedingly for your health.   If you have kept your letters for 'my sake,' for my sake do not be reckless of your precious life.   If you have devoted it to God, you ought to be careful to preserve it for him.   They tell me that you have the care of your sister's school, that most of the parochial duties done in the village devolve upon you.   It does not seem possible that a constitution no firmer than yours can long sustain so much labor.   It is not possible.   I supposed that if you were going to Exeter, it must have been in hope of securing more repose.   I am glad you are not going. I do not like to have you change, if change can be well avoided.   The Lord will guide you, I trust."

Mr. Smith replied to this, and she wrote, in answer, the following, dated Nov. 22, 1838 :

" MY DEAR SIR, — The time has at length arrived, when it becomes my privilege to sit down to reply to your letters, with feelings not altogether unlike those I was wont to experience in days long gone by, and lest I should omit some circumstances which I ought to mention, I will notice the several topics of your letters in their order.

" The subject of my first you will recollect.   I was greatly obliged to you for the promptitude and freedom with which you wrote as a pastor.   In respect to the facts you were pleased to communicate in the same letter relative to your situation at Woonsocket, I was more than 'not unwilling to excuse.' Every circumstance relating to your prosperity is interesting to me, you may be assured. I rejoice with you in the success which has attended you in your labors, and in the kindness which you have experienced. You will find devoted friends everywhere, I doubt not, and may the special blessing of God ever attend you.

"In relation to writing occasionally upon common subjects, I frankly own it impossible for me to write to you, or to read your communications without emotion. I have supposed your relations might be such as to render such correspondence highly inexpedient, if not dishonorable. Of the facts in reference to this point, I am profoundly ignorant. Report is often positive, and as often contradicted. However this may be, I appeal to you, if it is possible for you to be indifferent when writing freely? if so, I have altogether mistaken your character. I know the fondness with which the soul revels in its own miseries; but the banquet is deadly: one cannot thus indulge with impunity. As a Christian, how have I cherished your remembrance! It has often consoled me, that I should meet you in heaven, and that you would not frown upon me then. But the death-bed has been wrapped in darkness. How sad, that that agonizing moment should be embittered by the remembrance of injuries unforgiven! May kind heaven forbid it.

"Have you received my hasty note, sent by private hand? It was written very hurriedly. I hardly know what it contained. I suggested in it, however, that I should be glad to see you. It certainly seems very desirable that we should at least attempt to understand each other, and this can only be done, I feel confident, by a personal interview. Were you near, I should be happy to see you during the week of vacation, which I am to have very soon."

In January, Mr. Smith visited Miss Hazeltine at her home. It was then decided that they should be married the following spring or summer.

She writes to Miss Patterson, April 14, 1839: — "You have suspected me of mischief that I have been silent so long. Well, you have guessed quite right. I am to be married next August to my own dear J. So fate determines, and I do not repine. I have ever loved him, and to whom should one be married, but to the one she loves? So I am turning my face towards house-keeping and married life."

She writes to Miss H. H. Smith: — " I have just been reading your letters to me. And where do you think I found them? In a parcel with those of Misses P. R., S. A., P. P., Mrs. C., the Rev. G. F. D., and the Rev. B. J., all dead. Do not be startled; but was it not singular? *Just these* letters together, and no others! And yet I felt constrained to acknowledge that the association was not altogether unbefitting. I have delayed a long time to answer your last, of October 10, 1835, have I not? I never read it but once; it was *too kind;* and I put it away, it seems, with the relics of the departed. But, my dear girl, may I answer it *now?* Will a letter from Martha be

18*

acceptable *now?* As I read, I cannot help asking myself, Is Hannah still the same? I owe you a thousand thanks. You have fulfilled my last request; you will recollect it — in the note to which you refer in the letter before me. That you have done it for 'my sake,' I do not know. It is enough that you have *done* it. O, Hannah, how much I wish I could see you, and know that you *are*, what you *were*. I have pictured you otherwise; yet they tell me you yet speak kindly of me. What fearful mysteries do these last three years hold concealed! Mysteries, which each fears to ask, or to disclose.

"I hear very little from you, Hannah; only now and then a word by accident; for you know I cannot inquire, and all seem to think it would be impertinent to mention your name to me. If you feel disposed to give me some account of this strange oblivious period, it would afford me great gratification. But do not write me, Hannah, unless you love me still, for I could never bear to receive an indifferent letter from *you*."

The summer of 1839 was a very busy period to Miss H. She felt ambitious to close her public career with honor, and to anticipate everything necessary to make her transition to domestic life pleasant and appropriate. She found in Miss Mickell, an old pupil, and a very warm friend, a most efficient aid. For years previous to this, Miss M. had given her proof of a generous heart and a dignified taste, in her liberal and appropriate contributions to the Literary and Missionary Association. Miss H. now confided very much to her taste and arrangements, and the issue proved that she had selected a very devoted and constant friend.

Miss H. writes to Miss M., June 20 : — " Would you believe that I have been honestly endeavoring, ever since the reception of yours, to write you in reply, and have been absolutely unable to do it ? It is literally true, and I hope and trust you will extend charity, and exercise forbearance towards me, for this seeming neglect, instead of thinking me negligent or ungrateful. Accept my warmest thanks for the unprecedented interest you take in my welfare, and the personal sacrifices which you are so ready to make for my happiness.

" Come, my dear girl, and occupy my parlor, the week before the event in anticipation, if you can do so without inconvenience to yourself. It will be a great comfort to me to have you here, and we will try to make you just as happy as possible. Do you go to the mountains ? If so, do lay your plans to go in company with us. My kind regards to your brother. Please present him my most cordial invitation to be present at the wedding."

In giving an account of the renewal of her correspondence with Mr. Smith and her reëngagement of marriage, it is not necessary to present all the circumstances in detail ; it is, however, proper to state, that she had come to regard the discontinuance of the correspondence and engagement as decidedly *wrong*. To her dying day, however, she never reflected upon herself, as having erred, *consciously*, yet, she was con-

vinced she had erred *really ;* and deeply deplored the
decision, which, though made with the most *sincere*
and *ardent* desire to know and do her duty, had, notwithstanding, been, both to herself and her friend,
the cause of so much bitter sorrow.   From the time
of her reëngagement to Mr. S., it was evident that
the inward conflict of her feelings ceased.   Now all
within was peace.   Her cheerfulness became natural,
not artificial.   Imagination, tired, *tired* with her years
of wandering to and fro, returned to the ark, whence
she had escaped, and, though, at choice, "still free
to roam," yet gladly "folded her wings," and rejoiced
to find an entrance still open and a ready hand to
make her welcome.   To the latest period of life she
ceased not to give thanks to God that by his merciful providence He so ordered events as effectually to
heal her wounded heart, and secure the consummation of her earthly hopes.

CHAPTER XXII.

WE come now to speak of the time when Miss Hazeltine resigned the cares of school for the quiet of domestic life. She was married to the Rev. Joseph Smith, August 14, 1839. The period of her leaving school, she had anticipated, and provided for. She felt that she had left no effort untried to establish the seminary upon a firm basis, and that everything had been anticipated to secure its permanency.

The following extract from a letter, written a few months after her marriage, to her successor at New Hampton, will exhibit her feelings: — "I am happy, very happy. No beating blast has hitherto reached me. All is *quiet*, *peaceful*, and *pleasant*. I am determined to make the most of my retirement, and shut out the busy, bustling world as far as possible. One would think I designed to cut all ties of friendship, as well as of business, judging by my communications. The conclusion, however, would be most unjustly drawn in my case. If I say less, I think and feel more.

"I am glad all things move on so well at New Hampton, that you are sailing full and fair, God bless you. The society has my best wishes. I suppose you have not much news. There are certain general features in the seminary which are ever the same; certain slight and imperceptible changes, time is effecting with her accustomed adroitness, I suppose. Yet its identity remains, as does our own. May it long live, and become venerable with its age. And excuse me for adding, let it remain essentially unchanged. I love to contemplate it as it was, and to believe that such, in most respects, it still continues to be."

She writes to Miss Patterson, Jan. 23 : — "Be assured I am enjoying a full quota of happiness, and seem, alas! too little inclined to interest myself in the affairs which but so recently constituted my whole element. I seem to want to forget everything past, but a few choice friends. Would you believe that one to whom all have attributed so much ambition, should so *heartily loathe* the chase of fame! But so it is. Let those seek notoriety who find a pleasure in it; as for *me*, give me *quiet*; and this, you should share with me, if I could order your fortunes. It is *so good* to cast off the heavy yoke of public domination, and be sole mistress of a sweet little home, with the very inmates, whom of all in the world, one loves best.

"We have nothing here by way of news. One day is much like another; that is, in its general features. Now and then a day devoted to calls, a singing school once in a week, prayer meeting three evenings; one afternoon prayer meeting for females; sewing society once a month; calls in abundance every pleasant day; visits occasionally in neighboring villages. So judge if I am busy with these duties, together with doing daily the honors of my house."

She writes to Miss S., March 25th: — "You do not know how much I am disappointed that you are not to visit us soon. You have avoided saying a word upon the subject, with the design, I imagined, to give us the more agreeable surprise. I was looking for you, notwithstanding, this evening, as I thought that between the multitude of your business at home, and the loud calls abroad, you would strike the medium about this time. But as much as I am disappointed, I so heartily approve your plans that I cannot say a word.

"I am glad you are sufficiently devoted to the interests of New Hampton to invest moneys there in the purchase of a boarding establishment. I am glad for the seminary, which you must excuse me, if I still consider in some sense mine. Nor do I believe you will regret the measure. I think you will find it, in time, well invested money *literally*, as well as in a more liberal sense.

"I am glad your health is so good. You are so skilful in the matter of husbanding it well, that I hope it will not fail you soon. You must not presume, however, too much upon your good constitution; I know it promises much, but yet it *may* fail you, if too severely drawn upon. You must remember that many hopes hang upon you, and let this consideration modify your estimation of your own worth.

"And now, Sis, I must submit to you my communication for the report. Allow me to assure you I have done the best that I could, and cheerfully submit the result to your acceptance or rejection, it is the following : —

To the Acting Members of the Ladies' Literary and Missionary Association and Education Society of the New Hampton Female Seminary.

DEAR YOUNG LADIES, — You will recognise in the present communication the hand of our former Corresponding Secretary, addressing you, not as heretofore from the seat of studious halls, but from the quiet of domestic life. In view of this change, you perhaps would ask, if I still entertain my former sentiments upon the *constitution of human society and the mode of education best adapted to secure the ends of human life.*

Few subjects have afforded me more pleasure, as matters of speculation, than the *various relations which go to make up the tissue of human society.* Their mutual adaptation, their variety, their perfection and harmony, speak not only to the mind, but to the heart, and teach, in language too plain to be mistaken, the agency of an all-wise and supremely benevolent Being. There is perhaps no one accustomed to reflect, who may not have pursued this thought with greater or less satisfaction ; but I have been inclined to believe there is something in the experience of domestic life peculiarly adapted to it. It is here, indeed, we find the leading elements of society exemplified in fact, and subject to the closest observation. From the conjugal relation, involving in itself all that is tender in sentiment and delicate in action, we pass to the several affinities of kindred arising from it, and thence to the wide-extended, grand idea of human society.

Between this last idea and that of a domestic community well developed and regulated, the analogy is so exact and so full, that the question might naturally arise, whether it were not a part of the design of the domestic constitution to afford an illustration of it. Indeed, I think it doubtful whether, without such an aid, we should ever have been able to apprehend the idea, as recognised in the code of divine law. It is here we behold a great social brotherhood, whose primary relation to each other is that of strict equality, modified by the numberless variations of age, constitution, office and condition. Here, too, we see our common Father providing with equal care for the necessities of His children, and administering justice among them with parental impartiality and love.

Can anything be better fitted than such a view as this, to dispose our minds suitably towards every individual with whom we have to do? Could any one, with such impressions as it is adapted to inspire, deny to any member of the human family the rights of reciprocity and brotherly regard?

To impart correct views of the constitution of human society in its several departments, and of the laws which govern it, is a grand object of education. To this the efforts of the teacher should be directed,

19

as the mind of his pupil becomes gradually developed, commencing with those relations which are nearest and most easily understood, and proceeding to such as are less intimate and obvious. . Nothing will so effectually teach the mode of conduct proper to be pursued in our intercourse with the world, as a clear understanding of the relations it involves. All the practical maxims of life, however excellent, unless clearly perceived to have their origin in these relations, are adapted to act alone on minds essentially mechanical.

Such are the principles upon which the seminary with which this association is especially connected, has been, and I believe is still conducted. To develop well the mental faculties, so as to enable them to take a large and accurate survey of the wide field of observation ; — to direct the attention successively to the several departments within this range, and assist in gathering from each a store of general principles to be garnered in the mind for future use ; — to direct in the application of these principles to the conduct of human life, and in forming those habits which are to grow and strengthen with increasing years, and mould the character and destiny ; — these constitute the basis and almost the fabric of education.

And with such an education, young ladies, may we not venture to step forth upon the arena of social and domestic life ? Can. any change be rude or painful to us ? Have we not anticipated all ? We have not been trained merely to a round of habits. We have learned, I hope, to think and to reason.

We have learned to recognise the administration under which we live, and to interpret and apply its laws. We have accustomed ourselves to yield obedience to rightful and salutary authority. We are familiar with the necessities of real life, and have trained ourselves to meet them with cheerfulness. These things have become a second nature to us; what then have we to fear?

But I am extending my remarks too far. I could wish to say many things for your encouragement and profit, but the nature of this article forbids. You do not need to be reminded of what we were wont, when we associated together, habitually to inculcate and to study; — of the duty of *persevering* in every good enterprise; of doing everything from *principle*, and not from accident or caprice; — of extending the hand of *benevolent coöperation*, so far as practicable, to every one engaged in efforts for the general good; — of practising daily the gentle *virtues* which cluster round the shrine of *home*; and especially those dearer *christian charities* which your Heavenly Father loves. These are principles engraven not only upon your memory, but written in your hearts, and exemplified in your lives. The Lord bless you then, and enable you to press forward toward that perfection of character which is well pleasing in His sight, and to the full attainment of the christian hope.   **M. HAZELTINE SMITH.**

A little after, she writes to Miss S. again: — " You are disappointed that I do not manifest an enthusiasm equal to your own in the affairs of the seminary.

You must not expect it. I am a soldier, discharged, still too weary with fatigue and toil, to cast one *longing, lingering* look behind, though many a look of love and prayer escape me daily. Let me rest now, and, having resigned my charge, let my heart be at peace. May the Lord sustain *you* so long as he calls you to the arduous pursuit."

It might be inferred, from the preceding extracts, that when Mrs. Smith entered upon the duties of married life, she ceased from special efforts to be useful. This, however, was far from the fact. We have seen, that in her early history, that it was the ruling passion of Mrs. Smith to live for God, and to do good. That this was, with her, a fixed principle of action, is manifest, not less in her domestic, than in her public career. As soon as she was located at W. she asked, what the best good of those over whom she exerted an influence, demanded at her hands. The less informed needed to be instructed, and the intelligent to be perfected in the knowledge of the truth. This she attempted to do by forming a Bible class, and conducting it upon the same principle, (that of analysis,) that she had pursued in the class connected with the seminary over which she had had supervision. True, she could not gather around her a hundred young ladies, constantly devoted to the pursuit of knowledge, but she enlisted the interest of a large class, engaged in the common pursuits of life, and combined her energies in expanding their power of intellectual comprehension, and exciting a love for biblical truth.

To gain the sympathies and attention of the young,

she was accustomed to invite them to her home, professedly for the projection of sacred maps, but she had no less for her real object, biblical instruction. While she was teaching the various localities in sacred geography, she connected with them the accompanying history, and ere the children were aware, she had taught them to love to dwell upon the interesting incidents found in the Sacred Scriptures.

For the benefit and usefulness of the people, she enlisted her sympathies in charitable associations, originated plans, and sought out new means and new objects of benevolent enterprise. She was, during her whole life, a public servant. True, she was interested in home, and home duties; but whenever the wants and interests of others seemed to demand her energies, her own immediate interests became of secondary moment.

The class of mind upon which she acted at W. varied somewhat from that which she had been accustomed to influence at New Hampton, and perhaps, when she first entered upon her duties, she did not feel all that satisfaction from the result of her efforts which she had been accustomed to feel. But with her usual skill, she adapted herself to the wants of the people, and soon felt happy in the assurance that she was rendering herself useful and beloved. Though her passion for public usefulness did not change with the change of her situation, yet the elements of her religious character became evidently combined in juster proportions. She had ever, from the time of her conversion, been actively and zealously

engaged in the cause of her Divine Master. From
the time she took charge of the seminary, the spiritual welfare of her pupils, was even nearer her heart,
than their intellectual advancement. She heard and
prayed, and read so much with reference to them,
that she enjoyed even her own religion, less for herself than for others. She now felt, that God in his
providence released her from this load of responsibility, and before she attempted to enter upon the
more public duties of her new situation, she determined to devote herself especially to the work of examining her own heart, and laying anew, as it were,
the foundation of her hope. Faithfully did she do
this. The Bible, meditation and prayer, occupied a
large portion of her time, and the result was, a firmer
and more unwavering assurance than she had perhaps
ever before possessed.

CHAPTER XXIII.

PAINFUL as it is to trace the seeds of disease as they germinate and mature, there is, notwithstanding, a mournful pleasure in knowing all connected with those we love, even though there be scenes of anguish and pain.

It is supposed, both by friends and physicians, that the foundation of Mrs. Smith's disease was laid before she left New Hampton. She had a remarkably firm and vigorous constitution. But ten years of unremitted exertion as a teacher, and the painful incidents in her history, which had produced protracted and deep anguish of mind, could hardly fail to undermine the firmest constitution. Besides, just before she left the seminary, she was attacked with a disease common, as was supposed, to the season, which prostrated her system, and from which she was never afterwards entirely free. The excitement of closing her duties at New Hampton, and commencing anew in the midst of strangers, gave her no time immediately to regain her accustomed strength.

She was never perfectly well afterwards. New scenes, however, elasticity of spirits, and a *desire* and *resolve to be* perfectly well, induced her to believe that she was in good health, and that there was no excuse for less courage and activity than had formerly characterized her.

We have the first reference to declining health from herself, in a letter to Miss Mickell, dated Patterson, N. J., Aug. 10.

"You will wonder that I am here. We were desirous of making some tour for our health and the recreation of our spirits; and my husband receiving an invitation from the church in this place to spend some time with them, we made arrangements to be absent two sabbaths, designing to turn the time to as much account as possible. We came by way of Providence and New York, and have had, thus far, a delightful time. The scenery about this place is, as you are doubtless aware, highly romantic, embracing in close vicinity the falls of the Passaic. The cascade is, at this season, inconsiderable, as most of the water of the river is drawn off for the use of manufactories; but the rock scenery, which forms its bed, is grand. We visited it the next morning after our arrival, and were highly gratified. The religious interest here is much as at Woonsocket."

At one time, during their absence, the idea was strongly impressed upon her mind, that her death was near. It appeared at first to distress her, not that she feared to die, but her enjoyment of life was great, and she naturally regretted to leave it. She very soon, however, overcame this feeling, and realized that it was a blessed thing for the Christian to die, and that if such was her heavenly Father's will, she should be glad to go even then. Contrary, however, to her own expectation, she partially recovered, and, on returning to her home, resumed her duties in her family, in the social circle, and in her beloved Bible class. But though her strong resolution overcame, in a measure, her infirmities, her husband became sensible that her strength was gradually failing.

Sept. 11th, she writes to Miss Mickell: — "I returned from my journey in very bad health, supposing I should remain at home long enough to replenish my supply of apparel, and then take lodgings elsewhere in pursuit of better air and more constant medical attendance. But, as the kind providence of God would have it, my health suddenly improved to such a degree as to warrant my remaining at home. The medicine you sent me is doing me material benefit."

Nov. 2. To the same. "We had a good day yesterday. Received eight members to the fellowship of the church. My health has been much improved since my return from New York. Am suffering again slightly from bilious affection, but hope to obtain relief soon.

"In what terms can I adequately thank you for the shower of favors from your hand, now lying before me in the form of communications; not to mention the many highly valued testimonials of your affectionate regard which crown many a shelf in my cabinet. Everything from you is of the choicest selection, *always*. But the several articles, which make up your case parcel, were particularly valuable to me, from the circumstance of their peculiar acceptableness to my dear husband. The shells he admires. We have been studying them together. He has made everything else give place to these upon the mantelpiece in the drawing room. The volumes, too, were just the ones. I am seizing every moment that I can lawfully, to devote to them."

A few weeks after the date of the letter above, she went to pass a few weeks in Providence, in the family of Mr. Miller, and writes the following from Providence to her husband at W.: —

"My dear Husband, — You can easily fancy the luxuriant prospect which greets my eyes this glorious morning — but the question you are now desirous of having answered is, with what eyes I am able to view it. Through the goodness of my heavenly Father, I am enabled to derive pleasure from it, though my vision is too feeble to behold it steadily. But I will endeavor to give you an account, as particular and connected as I can, of my history, since you left me. That was Friday. The doctor came, and heard my whole story — inquired very particularly what I had taken for two days past as *diet*, but said little of medicine — remarked that he would leave me simply an anodyne for the night, would see me the next day and observe my complexion, and, in the meantime, would give my case the best reflection of which he was capable — bade me be of good courage, and said good evening. The next morning he called in haste, looked at my complexion, my tongue, my eyes, and gave me a recipe for the apothecary — observed incidentally something about the " torpid state of the liver " * — said he did not expect to produce any sudden change — that everything would depend upon the Divine blessing, but that he would do what he could. He told me to keep quiet, to lie down or sit up just as my feelings dictated — said he would see me again on Monday. I am now waiting his visit, in order to tell you what more he will say. I have slept a large proportion of the time since you left, and have been very stupid and disinclined to exertion when awake ; but have suffered much less pain than for some time before."

In the afternoon she writes — " My dear love, — The doctor smiled as he looked on me this morning, and said I looked bright. I told him I was writing to you, and desired to know what I should say to you. He said that I might say, that everything, thus far, had operated kindly, that he did not like to say much of the future, but hoped that he should be able to do me some good."

" I am afraid his remedies will act slowly, but if they act *effectually*, I ought not to be impatient. The doctor decidedly disapproves of violent exertion ; his great charge is, ' keep quiet.'

" I am afraid you had a dull day yesterday, there was so much snow. You could not hope to effect much in your peculiar province. But the Lord reigns, and it was of his providence that the assembly was small. I hope you realize every precious gospel motive to resignation and cheerfulness. I

---

* Her disease now was the apthoides chronica.

think of you all the time, dearest, but am by no means discontented. This is the very best place of all in the world for me to be in. I am becoming fatigued, dear, and I am sure you will excuse a short letter. The Misses Windsor send much love. They are doing everything for me. I am greatly indebted to *them*, as well as to Mrs. Miller.

"Dear love, accept the affectionate ' good night ' of your own dear

"MARTHA."

* "She was able at this time, to sit up most of the day, and enjoy reading and conversation, and for a week or two was very happy in the society of the kind Christian friends, who had thus hospitably received her. She, however, though not apparently worse, was evidently not gaining, as she had hoped. As her physician came to her one morning, about this time, she said, ' Doctor, I am almost discouraged; it seems as though I never should get well.' He replied that he could not encourage her, ' things do not take the course I wish, and I consider your case very doubtful; but it is safe to leave it in the hands of God.' She made no reply. The announcement had come suddenly, and she was evidently gathering up her strength to meet it. The doctor soon left, and her friends silently and tearfully withdrew. When they were alone she said to her husband, ' This news is sudden, dearest, is it not?' He merely said, ' Yes,' for it was indeed sudden to him.

* From an obituary notice.

She appeared to be for a little time revolving the subject in her thoughts, and then having grasped the idea in its full force, and felt its solemn influence, she immediately began to make preparation for the event, by attempting a disposition of her affairs. But she was to weak to do much, and after some little effort desisted.   She then said, 'Well, dear one, you have for a little time smoothed my path. I have never known sorrow since I became your wife. You healed my heart, though you cannot heal my body. And now I go to prepare a place for you, or rather to welcome you to a place already prepared. I have welcomed you many times on earth, and how sweet to think that I may be permitted to welcome you to heaven.' The remainder of this day and the next, the idea that she was soon going home, was thus present with her, and though her weakness and the intensity of her suffering were such as to prevent her saying much, it was evidently pleasing. Her friends, however, were not yet prepared to relinquish her, and a consulting physician was called, and though he gave little hope, both agreed, that the most favorable symptom of her case was her great resolution, which was especially remarkable in this disease, as it usually prostrates the powers of the mind quite as rapidly as those of the body.   In order, therefore, to keep up the hope of recovery as long as it could be of any use, effort was made to call off her thoughts from dwelling so entirely on the prospect of death, and win her back to earth.

She was still able to sit up two or three hours of the day, and to enjoy the reading of the bible, but owing to her constant and distressing pain, could converse very little. She now returned, as it were, to life. Her mind, at short intervals, appeared to act with more energy even than in health. Any idea that took possession of it was immediately carried to an extreme, and she now became anxious to get well, and sanguine in the hope that she should do so. It having been suggested that if she were able to be removed to Newport, the air of that place might assist her recovery, she became exceedingly urgent to be carried there, insisting that she was perfectly able to bear it, although she had become so weak as to be unable to be raised without fainting. This was perhaps ten days previous to her death. She now sunk rapidly, and her friends relinquished all hope of her recovery; but as it had been necessary, from the nature of her complaint, to keep her almost constantly under the influence of opium, it was difficult to make her understand her situation. Saturday morning previous to her death, as she had been able to get through the night previous with a smaller quantity of laudanum than usual, she was more in possession of her faculties. She was asked if she knew how low she was. She replied, 'I see you are discouraged, but why? am I so much worse?' She was then told distinctly that the physicians could do nothing more for her, and she would probably live but a few days. As she made no reply, her husband asked if she feared death. 'O no,' said she, 'I should be delighted to die — delighted to die — but I don't like to make up my mind that I am going to die, and then come back to think I shall get well — this

change is painful.' She was asked if she wished to send messages to any of her friends. She said, ' Yes, a great many.' Miss Sleeper was particularly mentioned, and she said she wanted to say a great deal to her. Their connection, for many years, had been such, that it would be a solemn thing to take leave of her. ' But,' said she, ' I do not yet realize that I am going to die. I must think more about it, and bring death nearer to me, and then I will tell you what I wish to say.' Some time after this, she requested that she might be left alone. One of her friends, who was not quite well, as she was sitting out of her view, and therefore would not disturb her, remained. When she thought herself alone, she called upon God to sustain her, in these words: —
' O Lord, I would lift up my prayer to thee at this solemn period; now, when flesh and heart fail me, be thou my strength. O awaken me, arouse me from this lethargy, this torpor that pervades my powers, and let me prepare to die. O come quickly — come quickly and release me. O give me strength — give me strength — arouse me from this stupidity; and as I can no longer serve thee actively, O help me to honor thee in my sufferings. O hast thou not been precious to my soul, in days that are past — have I not tasted that thou art gracious — O Lord."
After this her words were inaudible, and she soon became exhausted, and lay for a few minutes quiet. Her sister then came to her, and she said, ' Read to me.' ' Where shall I read ?' Why, you know where — *In my father's house are many mansions.*'

Sabbath morning, she uttered a few words of prayer,

and expressed her determination to devote the day
as far as possible to self-examination. She told
Mr. S. what messages she wished to send to the
church at W., of which he was that day to take
his leave as pastor. She was not able to converse
much after this; but once during the day, expressed
her sorrow that she had relied too much upon means,
for the recovery of her health. She felt that she had
not leaned simply upon God in this matter as much
as she ought. Monday was a day of intense suffering, and no attempts were made to talk with her. In
the evening she expressed a most affectionate and
earnest desire to see Miss Sleeper. Tuesday morning this wish was gratified. 'I thank God I see you
before I die,' was first whispered from the lips then
touched with death. Then she returned the kiss of
love, which showed that her heart still beat true to
friendship. One, who for eleven years had received
from her demonstrations of tender affection, who for
seven had been an associate teacher, and a constant companion, could not but recall past scenes
of interest and moment. Though her system was
perfectly prostrated by disease, and her senses be-
numbed by powerful specifics, for a time the mind
seemed to act with its accustomed vigor, and the
thoughts to flow in their usual channel. In the
course of the morning she referred most satisfactorily
to the prominent scenes of her past life.

Her feelings, in view of eternity, spoke volumes
upon the value of the principles of the Gospel. No
one could have heard her converse without feeling
that it is the true philosophy, as well as a required

duty, to live entirely for the glory of God. To labor unremittingly for the good of others, irrespective of personal emolument and of the spirit in which instructions may be received. 'O, how differently I should live and labor,' she exclaimed, 'if I could live with the views I now have. The salvation of the soul would be my all-absorbing theme. I would teach, but then how differently I would teach. I do not know that I would teach a ladies' seminary. I should fear the effects of ambition. I would teach children — the mind is then susceptible, and I would have for my object, what is the proposed object of the Sabbath School. Science and literature unsanctified are no blessings. All teachers have a very important situation. They are educating souls for eternity. Do be careful, my dear sister, to inculcate right principles, to present laudable aims.'

When asked if, with her present views, she would have the plan of the seminary, over which she had so long presided, materially changed, she replied, she thought not. All she should fear, would be the acquisition of knowledge from wrong motives, or of giving an undue amount of time to those branches which ought always to be subordinate. She felt that there was a liability for accomplishments to engross too much time, and a temptation to study from motives of ambition, or a desire to display. These she would have strongly guarded against.

She felt that common schools deserved a higher rank than she had been accustomed to give them — that the rich field of influence they presented, ought to claim the efforts of elevated minds. Early youth, she felt emphatically to be the time, when the mind must be acted upon by those who would labor most successfully in fitting souls for heaven. She seemed, too, to feel that the comparatively little temptation to the teacher to labor for the applause of the world, or self-aggrandisement, was a great recommendation to it as a situation for the employment of young ladies. She now feared that while she had labored extensively for the good of others, she had really been endeavoring to serve herself. She believed that she had been too anxious to gain the approbation of the world, too sensitive concerning the world's estimation of her character. She would have then impressed upon her pupils to be solicitous only for their duty to God and to others, and fearlessly to perform it.

She felt also that there was danger of exercising entirely wrong feelings towards those who had injured us. It had been difficult for her to exhibit cordiality and kindness toward those who had injured her, until concessions had been made. But she now felt that she could love and desire the happiness of all irrespective of their feelings towards her. 'O,' said she, 'I have needed this long term of sickness to elevate my affections, and teach me how to live acceptably unto God.'

When asked if she then felt prepared to die, she replied, 'essentially.' She lamented that she had not realized sooner her approaching end, that everything might have been prepared. She trusted that she might hope for happiness beyond the grave. She felt a degree of confidence in trusting herself to the Saviour, although she had not so bright an evidence, so ecstatic joy, as she would have desired.

When asked what word she would leave for those who had been her pupils, she replied, 'I wish I could convey to them my present view of the world and its blandishments; that I could impress upon them the invaluable excellences of religion in view of eternity, and the way to live that they may die in peace. But I am too weak, I can think very little connectedly. I fear for them.'

This was her last connected conversation. Tuesday afternoon she grew very much weaker, and although most of the time apparently rational, she took very little notice of anything passing around her, or hardly uttered a connected sentence. Several friends called. She uniformly recognised them, but was too weak to say more than that she knew and loved. Friends seemed a support to her to the very last. Her husband was constantly by her, and received every proof that he was her greatest earthly solace.

Wednesday and Thursday she frequently seemed in a happy frame of mind, and exhibited the feeling by some exclamation as — precious religion — it is delightful. Both Wednesday and Thursday her husband prayed with her at her request, and she seemed to join in the prayer and enjoy it. Thursday, about three o'clock, we perceived the closing scene of life fast approaching. Her breathing became difficult, her eyes turned from side to side; she continued in this state until after seven in the evening. Her eyes then gradually ceased to move, her breathing changed to short and distant respirations, her pulse became less and less perceptible, the beating of the heart fainter and fainter, until the breath ceased forever. We then all knelt in the presence of Him who has the life of all in his hands, while the afflicted, yet divinely supported husband, asked that the dispensation might be sanctified, and that we might all feel that the afflictive stroke was from Him, who is too wise to err and too good to be unkind."

Her physician wrote the following to her husband the next morning:—"My Respected Friend—I have received thy very kind note of this morning, and can hardly forbear saying to thee that thou hast my deepest sympathy. I know that words avail but little on an occasion like the present. I do not mean to intrude them upon thee—but having been in my time made to drink of a similar cup, I think I can *feel* for thee, and comprehend to some extent the desolation of thy heart; and yet, my friend, how full of comfort and consolation are the promises and hopes of the gospel on which I doubt not thou art permitted confidingly to rest. We do indeed know that for such as thy dear and excellent wife there is a building prepared of God, a house not made with hands, eternal in the heavens."

To the same, from Mrs. Brown, New Hampton:—"Forgive me, my dear brother, if I too soon intrude upon the sacredness of your sorrow. It is with no ordinary feelings that I address you, not to suggest topics of consolation, or to repeat the stereotype phrases of such occasions; but to mourn with you, to mingle my tears with yours over the dear departed, whose loss in this world can never be repaired.

" I have ever felt thankful that, in the midst of her soul's deep trouble, I was permitted to administer, though in a small degree, the consolations of friendship. To you, my brother, it must be a source of melancholy satisfaction, that you were allowed to smooth her passage to the tomb. To have won the love and confidence of such a woman, I consider no common honor ; to have enjoyed the fruition of that love, though but for a short period, no common bliss. That love and honor were yours; yours too, when she stood upon the proudest pinnacle of her fame, and men of prouder name and higher pretensions would have gloried in that love.

" I did hope at the time she united her fate with yours, though I saw too plainly the ravages which care and sorrow had made upon her once vigorous constitution, that the elasticity, imparted by hope and joy, would restore her to perfect health, and that she would long live, a blessing to you and to the world. But your companion has been removed. It has not, however, been without the permission of her Heavenly Father. He loved her even more than yourself, and transplanted her with his own hand to a more genial clime. But though for a while veiled from our sight, if we walk in her footsteps we shall soon be where sickness, anxiety and separation can never come. Yes, my afflicted brother, she will not return to you, but you will go to her. Shall we not look forward with still greater desire toward that Heaven where the dearest and best of earth are being gathered ? I cannot think of her as in the darkness and corruption of the grave. No; all too bright and pure, as she was, for this world, she has gone to that hallowed place of rest where the taint of earth, which could not but cleave to her here, has been removed. May you, my dear brother, not merely be supported under this great affliction, but be so forwarded by it in your Christian course, that you may have reason to bless God to the day of your death, not only that he gave, but also that he has taken away this precious one."

From the Clergyman who officiated at her Marriage Ceremony.

NEW HAMPTON, Feb. 27, 1841.

My heart is distressed for thee, my brother, and though my dear wife has already written, I cannot do justice to my feelings without pouring them out also in my own way. Yet what can I say that has not occurred to your own soul already. Let me at least sympathize, where I cannot instruct. Let me bear a brother's burden with him, and so fulfil the law of Christ.

I think I am not wholly ignorant of your feelings. As I rejoiced with you in the day of your espousal, in the season of the gladness of your heart, let me now weep with you over the tomb where those joys are buried — where the hand that then clasped yours in the warmth of wedded love, now lies mouldering in dust. O, the crushed hopes that died with her ! O, the pangs that will thrill a thousand bosoms, when they hear that she, their teacher and friend, is no more — that she who had twined herself around their "heart of hearts," is passed away from earth in the brightness of her years! It is not wrong to mourn her loss, though our loss be her gain. "Jesus wept." Devout men bore Stephen to his burial, "and made great lamentation over him." Our tears are told in heaven; nor till we reach that happy world, will they be for ever wiped away. Let them flow then over even "the blessed dead." The spontaneous tribute of affection to departed worth, they relieve the full heart, that yet would not murmur at the removal of a gift so precious. If self-abasement say, "I was not worthy to enjoy it longer," let the same spirit add, "Blessed be the mercy that gave it me at all!"

To you, in this affliction, I know all things are changed. The fond ambition, silently, unconsciously nursed in early years, is indeed, I doubt not, perished in her grave. You feel like one just rising from the billows that have rolled over him, and wrecked him on a strange and inhospitable shore. You seem to cast your eyes for the first time on the world, as on an immeasurably wide, bleak, and sterile waste. Perhaps there are moments when you feel as if now that she is gone, you were strangely cut off from the whole living creation — as if none could thoroughly sympathize with you in a grief so profound and peculiar in all its circumstances — as if there was no warmth of heart (now that one warm heart is cold,) remaining upon earth. All your past experience of pain may seem to you as nothing compared with this one overwhelming visitation — as if for the first time you had awaked from the dreams of the night to the stern reality of woe.

I recall these melancholy ideas that I may assure you I sympathize with you in them — partially at least — though it has never been my lot to go through *all* that you have been called to endure. Be it so, my brother! Yet I persuade myself, from my knowledge of your christian principles, that you have not found this cup one of unmingled bitterness. No, there was no curse in it! You have been drawn to Jesus by this affliction. He has supported you, in your long struggle, and in your bitter desolation. He has assured you of His unalterable love. He has soothed the convulsive agony of your spirit. He has given you the victory over a dying world. What moments of sacred peace! What emotions of heavenly elevation! What lessons of divine wisdom! What new and ennobled acts of self-consecration to Himself and to His cause, has He inspired!

You will go to Newport alone — and yet not alone — surely He whom your soul loveth above all, will be with you there. You will go desolate, but I trust more humbly and exclusively devoted to Christ and the welfare of souls. You will go there not to enjoy, so much as to act — to enter into the wants of dying men, and into the sorrows of the afflicted — comforting those that are cast down with the comforts you have yourself received of God. You will go where the excellent Clark and Holmes — names embalmed in the history of the church — labored in darker days than ours — labored, and did not faint. May you drink deeply into their spirit! May you be a worthy successor to those blessed men, and reap largely the fruit of your toils.

I am glad our dear sister is to be buried in Mount Auburn. It is a place befitting her public character and extended usefulness — unless indeed she were buried *here*. In the sweet language of the present Mrs. Judson,

> " Wilt thou not kneel beside the sod
>   Of her who kneels with thee no more,
> And give thy heart anew to God,
>   To Him who griefs unnumbered bore ? "

Forgive this strange, erratic letter, which I write in much confusion, and assure yourself of the daily sympathies and fervent prayers of

Your affectionate brother in Christ,

J. NEWTON BROWN.

From Miss Mickell.

I thank God for bestowing upon my ever-to-be-lamented friend and teacher so much grace and strength, as the words you gathered up during her approaching dissolution exhibited. Surely, my dear brother, there is *much* that is alleviating and mitigating in this trial of our faith — many soothing considerations. Her life, while it was given her here, was *full* of usefulness far above her cotemporaries ; her days of sojourn were days of virtue, of *deep-toned* piety ; and their close, peaceful, happy ! With assurance of glory and immortality beyond !

O ! may this event of Providence be sanctified to us all, and especially to you, and to those who have been under the immediate influence of her indefatigable labors. She was a *chosen* vessel, and *well* has the pleasure of the Lord prospered in her hands.

The scraps of prayer and ejaculation you mentioned, give me great satisfaction. And any farther particulars that may occur to your mind, I shall deem it a privilege and a delight to hear. O! ever shall I love to talk of her who has stood so long preëminent in my earthly attachments.

Is it not consolatory to feel that our bereavement comes not from the dust, is not the result of a random chance, but the will of our heavenly Father? And I trust we have not a wish or a hope but that he should do as it seemeth good unto him. I do feel that I know that measure of excellence in your wife as enables me to *estimate* your affliction, and deeply to lament, that a companion so profitable, was not permitted you longer in the pilgrimage of life. But this affliction may strongly exemplify the truth that whom the Lord loveth he chasteneth. God's ways are not our ways, nor his thoughts our thoughts. In his unerring wisdom, this grievous event was known to be salutary, or it never would have been permitted. O that we may be even willing to *suffer* the will of our heavenly Father, as well as to do it. We will not look for *unmingled* joy in this world, but prepare to take life as others have taken it, light and darkness, sunshine and shade, pain and pleasure, good and evil. And when bereavements are common in our day, O, shall we look upon them as *strange* things, and not *rather* as the appointment of a gracious God. Rather ought we to rejoice that they are so few and alleviated; that they are founded in love to our souls, and designed to make us richer partakers of a life of joy, which hath *no* sorrow. And whatever be the trial, that we are called to bear, O, may we remember to look before and see our blessed Lord bearing a much greater, and for us; and bearing it without sorrow or murmuring!

I trust you will not be displeased, when I tell you I have felt it a privilege to sympathize outwardly as well as heartily with your friends, by putting on the habiliment of mourning for the departed. But oh! how does my heart grieve at *every* instance of recollection! How much I had hoped in her improving society, with my restored health; and purposed many changes for her approving eye. But she mingles in brighter scenes, and I would not, if I could, constrain her unbound spirit into bonds again.

O, let us be thankful for the portion of her life that has been allowed us, and be *ever* submissive to the Divine will.

From Miss Patterson.

Lūnenbūrg, August 23, 1841.

Rev. Mr. Smith,

Dear Sir,—I cannot do myself the injustice to refrain from adding my humble testimony, to the worth of your lamented wife. For a number of years, as you are well aware, I shared largely in her confidence and affection; and my heart tells me the void that her decease has made will not be easily filed.

In 1831 I became a member of the New Hampton Female Seminary, and my acquaintance with this dear friend commenced at that period. The sentiment that predominated in my feelings towards her, for some months after I first saw her, was *admiration* of her talents and acquirements. As one of many who had equal claims upon her, as a teacher, I had no opportunity of knowing her in any other capacity. The goodness of her heart, and the soundness of her judgment, I had no reason to question, but at the time of which I speak, these were lost to me, in the brilliancy of her literary powers, which were then far below the acme of her subsequent attainments. Her taste was classical and chaste, she excelled in literary criticism, and was uniformly just. She sought to balance the defects she found in any production, by collecting all its beauties, and arranging them in their most attractive light. Her talent for communication was a happy one, she was emphatically, "apt to teach," her ideas being clothed in language most appropriate. Of her qualifications as a teacher of French, a French lady, of whom I took lessons after having been under her instruction nearly a year, bore very complimentary testimony, by doubting my assurance that I had never been taught by any one except an American. She observed, that "she had had a hundred pupils, who had brought the pronunciation of their various teachers, not one of whom had been taught so correctly as myself."

She was, I believe, as much at home in other languages. You may recollect that some time ago she took lessons in Hebrew, in a class of professional gentlemen. Professor S. remarked to a friend of mine, that "she was the best scholar in his class." This was a gratuitous tribute to her talents, for when he made the observation, it was to a lady in Ohio, a perfect stranger to your wife. But why need I dwell on this part of her character? It is less the splendor of her intellectual powers, than her qualities of heart, that embalms her memory. Happy, indeed, are her friends, that they can truly say of her, *she was as good as she was great.*

While a member of the seminary, sickness and sorrow laid a heavy hand upon me; then I began to test the generosity of her nature. She usually met me with a kind word, and always seemed fully to compassionate my inability to apply myself to study, as my associates did. I have often wondered, how one, who knew only the elasticity of feeling attendant on uniform health, could so justly appreciate the capabilities of an invalid. Our intimacy did not assume the character of confidential intercourse, until I decided to leave New Hampton for the seminary at Troy, New York. A few days before I left, she invited me to her room, and proffered me the warm and sympathizing heart of a friend. The offer was gladly accepted, and from that time our mutual confidence and affection was on the increase. Our correspondence bears ample testimony, that we shared each other's joy and grief, and is so personal in its character, that I cannot persuade myself to offer but very few letters for the examination of her biographer.

There was one feature in her character that always pleased me very much — something like the

21*

simplicity of childhood. She would often throw off
all reserve, and exhibit a gaiety of feeling, the spontaneous gushing of a joyous heart, such as few retain
after having become engrossed in the business of life
When the green sward, the "may-flowers and violets,
the robins and the wrens," succeeded the snows and
whistling winds of winter, she seemed animated to a
buoyancy of spirit like that of youth's bright morn.
Her cares were all forgotten; and her thoughts,
chastened by religious sentiment, after revelling for
a time among the beauties of creation, would soar,
"through nature up to nature's God." But what I
remember of this loved and lost one, with the greatest
pleasure, is the consistency of her christian character,
and the extent of her salutary influence. "Many
daughters have done virtuously," but in looking over
the circle of my acquaintances, my heart bears testimony, that justice compels me to say of her, "yet
thou excellest them all." It is useless to attempt a
computation of the good she has done in raising the
standard of female education and excellence, to say
nothing of the still greater good, in planting religious
principle, and forming christian character. Eternity
alone will reveal the truth, and so inadequate am I
to the task of enumerating her excellences, that I
choose to leave their development to that great day,
when in the presence of countless myriads I trust to
hear the Saviour say of her, "she has done what she
could," while he welcomes her to the joys of the
Lord.

I have, my dear sir, expressed only a tithe of the
tender recollections of your beloved wife, which I

love to cherish. Her works praise her more than can any testimony of friends. and with these you are well acquainted. If there is anything in this communication, or in the few letters which I have selected from her correspondence, that will add to the interest of her biography, you are at liberty to use both as you please.

While you are the greatest sufferer in this afflictive dispensation of Providence, there are many hearts that mourn sincerely with, and for you. May you find this sore trial among the "*all things*" that a kind heavenly Father sees for your good.

From Mrs. E. L. Magoon.

I *did love* your wife, my affectionate teacher and friend, with a strength that years have not lessened, nor death destroyed. I was under her immediate instruction four academical years; and I feel conscious that much, very much of the character I possessed as a scholar was owing to the inspiration and love of study received from her. And more than all, in the station I now occupy, I am constantly made to feel, that under God, to her I owe my fitness for public duties, and all the ability I possess, however large or small it may be, to be the companion of a minister of the gospel. Scarcely a day goes over me in which some principle that she implanted in my mind is not called into practice. I do not mean to arrogate to myself the honor of having made attainments, or of possessing characteristics not common to all her pupils; but I do mean that she inspired ALL WHO WOULD BE INSPIRED with a desire of excellence, that few who were never under her instruction have ever felt. This is obvious from the fact, that all who were her pupils for any considerable length of time, have been enabled to take an elevated position both as scholars and Christians. I recollect well how she used to draw forth the hidden energies of the timid and retiring; inspiring them with confidence and leading them on until their future progress was rendered certain by the living, burning desire for knowledge, which she had created within them.

But I must push back the memories which come crowding upon me. When visiting New England I was gratified to learn, from one who assisted to smooth her dying pillow, the details of her last hours. At New Hampton I felt it to be a privilege to meet the friends of former days, in mutual sympathy and united testimonies of regard for the dead — so much lamented. And more than all it was to me a sad and mournful pleasure to seek out her last long home in that "city of the dead," Mount Auburn, and stand by the side of her tomb. I never knew her but in the flush of health; could it be I stood above her decaying, crumbling body? I could not realize it, and though tears dropped upon the sods under which she quietly rests, yet I half thought her still living. And does she not live? Yes, truly. Even on earth she yet lives in the influence exerted by the large number of pupils who drank rich drafts of wisdom from her lips, and are now dispersed abroad as blessings to society.

From Miss Mickell.

May we not behold, in the numberless mirrors of nature, the manifest presence of Him who filleth "all in all"? In them does he not commune with those children of his love, that lift the adoring eye? And is it not true that when we suffer our affections to be elevated in gratitude and love to our God, we find great alleviation in our *disappointed hopes*, and *painful deprivations?* In Him is fulness of joy. He is *ever* with us, protecting our sleeping pillow, guarding our daily path, and fostering all our holy aspirations! How precious are the promises of our holy religion! Amid the vicissitudes and uncertainties of life, the heart is insecure in the possession of its most happy earthly creations. O! how often, how very often is it, in an unforeseen moment, brought to despondency upon its bereavements! But if our afflictions are measured in the light in which our infinite Father condescends to place them, we shall find them ever essential to our happiness and eternal interest. I have heard it said, and I think it a beautiful remark, that "Afflictions from above are angels sent on embassies of love, to pluck our flowers of hope from the earth, and plant them high on yonder sky, transformed to stars and fixed in heaven."

How true is it of our loved and ascended one — blessed spirit! With the songs of the seraphim, and the rich harmonies that arise from angel lyres, *loud and clear among them all are the strains of that newly strung harp,* joining the unceasing song, "to God and the Lamb."

O ! God forbid that we should beckon her away.
Better, my brother, that we earnestly employ ourselves to secure the end of our being, so *perfectly
attained* by her whom we have loved so well, and
who, by our heavenly Father's will, has entered upon her eternal rest.

Fresh in life is her precious memory, and it touches
upon the inmost recesses of the heart.   Yes, she was
worthy ; and she possessed all the excellences of our
nature.   And so beautifully combined with holiness
and truth !   Sweet were the tones of her earthly
harp — they were touched by Piety's soft hand, —
and hung upon Religion's shrine, and vibrated with
a sweet and solemn sound upon the ear of God.
I do love thus to contemplate, in my undisturbed
moments, my departed friend and teacher.

The following tribute to her memory is from the closing part of a
Discourse, delivered by Dr. Sharp, at Providence, R. I., Feb
21st, immediately after her interment.

The deceased was endued with an uncommonly
active and highly cultivated mind.   In early life she
gave signs of future eminence.   Although she was
not surrounded by the influences of a polished or
literary society, yet self-moved, she resolved to
enlarge her sphere of knowledge.   To accomplish
this noble purpose, she surmounted obstacles, submitted to sacrifices, and seized opportunities of study
with an avidity and resoluteness equalled by few.
Although not inspirited and encouraged by a class of
young ladies pursuing the same studies and urging
each other on, yet such was her unconquerable deter-

mination to be a scholar, that she became thoroughly acquainted with the Greek and Latin, and with the French and Italian, if not with some other modern languages.

Nor was she merely a scholar. She was a philosopher. She had not only the knowledge which memory accumulates, she had the superior attainments which can only be acquired by accurate observation, just comparison, clear discrimination, and protracted attention and reflection. She was at home in political economy, and in intellectual and moral philosophy. She led her pupils over the severe pages of logic — the still higher walks of sacred literature — and the flowery fields of rhetoric.

I must say, that I have never witnessed more thorough or satisfactory examinations at any institutions, literary or theological, than I have for several years in succession, at the female seminary over which she so successfully presided. She particularly excelled not only in imparting information, but in calling into action the perceptive and reflective powers of her pupils. She engaged the attention, and so roused the minds of the young, as to incite them to think for themselves.

Such was the intellectual and moral character of the teacher and of her instructions. She exerted an elevating influence from year to year, over the minds and habits of hundreds of young ladies, a large number of whom being teachers, are centres of intellectual influence in different and distant states of the Union. In our own New England, in the Middle States, and at the South and West are those who are transfusing the literary spirit which they received, in that remote but endeared spot, where they listened to the kind and intelligent lips of the deceased, surrounded by the rough but sublime mountain scenery of New Hampshire.

That I may not be considered as employing the terms of exaggeration, allow me to say, that one of the first belles-lettres scholars in our country, assured me the other day, that he had read some of the Reports of the New Hampton Institution, and had been delighted with the perusal ; adding, I know of no school for young ladies of a character so high and excellent.

But that which gave peculiar excellence to the instructions of Miss H., was the union of moral and religious with literary and scientific teaching. She was herself a Christian. She had a clear and comprehensive view of the relations of human beings to their Maker, and to one another, and she was not ashamed to avow and to teach her views. She felt an intense solicitude for the spiritual welfare of her pupils. She addressed them in public, she conversed with them alone in private. She prayed with and for them ; and in these her efforts she was greatly blessed. Perhaps it may not be too much to say, that during the whole period of her connection with that seminary, over one hundred pupils were indebted to her as the instrument of their salvation. Eternity alone can disclose the full and blessed amount of her labors.

How mysterious are the ways of Providence, that one so gifted and so useful, should be so suddenly, and to our limited comprehension, so prematurely removed to another world. We doubt not, however, that in this as in other inscrutable events, the designs of Providence are just, and wise, and good. Although some here were not prepared to lose her, it must be their great consolation that she was prepared to leave them, and to exchange earth for heaven. In view of her death, I have several times found myself repeating a line of Young's —

" That life is longest, which answers life's great end."

If that sentiment be true, of which we can have no doubt, our departed friend has lived a long life, and has now entered on the rewards of a blessed immortality.

From Miss Richardson, teacher at New Hampton, to Miss Sleeper, soon after the death of Mrs. Smith.

How in the spirit of prophecy was your remark, in the obituaries of last year's Report, that " soon our dearest and best would be in heaven." How emphatically has it been fulfilled. She, who labored with unremitted ardor to give character to our Society, who watched over its infancy, and encouraged its earliest attempts to acquire strength, has been removed to a society where labor, watching and anxiety, are exchanged for holy joy and perfect bliss. Not long truly did *she* " wait to join our dear ones " in that upper and better world. The sainted band of the early departed is fast swelling; louder do they strike their harps, and with greater rapture sing their praises at every instance of conquest over death. There is bitterness with us who remain, that so sweet flowers should be thus early gathered. But God does all things well, and in him who is "too wise to err and too good to be unkind," we may safely trust.

From Miss L. H. Freeman, formerly Teacher in the Seminary at New Hampton.

Can it be, that our dear Mrs. M. Hazeltine Smith is numbered with the dead? That her career of active effort and usefulness is ended? That we shall no longer hear her pious counsels, and feel the influence of her prayers? The sad intelligence is too well confirmed to admit a doubt; and we must confess, though with bleeding hearts, that the Judge of all the earth does right. While we deeply feel the loss of one so justly dear to her pupils and friends, we cannot but rejoice that she has left so shining an example of a piety, deep, ardent and consistent, that it will not be easily forgotten. How much good she has been the means of doing to the souls of others! How many, we have reason to believe, will rejoice through eternity that they were brought under her influence! We cannot calculate the amount of good one devoted Christian may accomplish; but we know it is infinite, both in extent and duration.

———◆———

IN MEMORY OF MRS. M HAZELTINE SMITH.

They may cull
The flowers of earth to decorate the name
Of the beloved dead; Music may breathe
Its tenderest dirges; and Affection come
With every offering, to enhance their praise;
But, is it well? Idolatry, perchance,
Itself enshrineth oft among the bowers

Where loveliest earthly things attract the heart
With fair, unsafe delusions, and enchain
Affection unto sense. O blessed few,
Whom the true spirit hath, by loveliness
Of natural beauty, led unto the pure
And everlasting, spiritual joys!
   But, Heaven, methinks thy beauty were divine,
And full and faultless, for my panting heart,
Were not a vision of one glorious scene
Before me, save the face of Jesus!

There,

In the clear radiance of His eye, the forms
Love deemed so beautiful, ere they put on
Their immortality, are bowing now,
With the gift-crowns! They turn not to behold
A heavenly good, that is not by His smile
Arrayed. Sense hath no joy but to exist
For ever in His light; and love is nought
To bind or bless their own united souls,
But, to be one in Him.

Went the rash eye

Upon forbidden errand, when it sought
The meeting of that fair, adoring band
Before the Saviour? Sorrow was half loth,
While His selecting hand, from clime to clime,
Passed, gathering up the rarest of His own;
Yet, toward one central star still every eye
Turned in its tears, as if that were the last
To darken and depart. But suddenly
From mid a wailing of the desolate,
Deeper than grief had tried, that guiding light
Stood with the band above.

Do they forget

The holy friendship, nourished 'mid these scenes
Of our delight — with the sad memory
Of their own smile, so dear and lovely now?
Nay, but their greeting, not as oft before,
Saith, " Welcome to my heart." A tuneful name,

Too glorious for a rival love, becomes
The first and only song. And every voice
Utters the name!   And every eye is turned
Upward to Jesus!

                O how beautiful
Were earthly things if lingering mourners now
Might find, in every relic of a friend,
And each familiar scene, some trace of Him
Who is the *all* of Heaven!

                    And memory,
Even, methinks, for ever might adore
The blessed name, for the great treasures gained
In discipline and conflict — when the grace
Of Jesus wrought salvation!   They have turned,
That happy band, their own high praises oft,
On victory in Him. ———— Who would prefer
Mere sympathies of human love, so sweet,
And so enrapturing?   Nay, it is not well!

O for a harp tuned to the harmony
Of that one only name!   O for an eye
Single to the Redeemer!   Then were all
Our sainted ones reflecting unto us
His own pure glory, and Himself indeed
Our only Heaven!

                               M. L. R

————◆————

LITERARY ARTICLES FROM THE PEN OF MISS H.

" The mines of science glitter in thy sight;
  Come dig for gems; thou may'st, 'tis woman's right;
  Set them in pearl, and with them crown thy brow;
  Thou might'st not always; but thou may'st now."

The present era is one in which, as females,
may well rejoice.   The shadows, which have so lo
brooded darkly over our destiny, are at length retre
ing before the bright dawn of christian philanthro
During the lapse of nearly six thousand years, t

true character and rank of woman have scarce been acknowledged. It is difficult to trace her history through this fearful period, without feeling deeply wounded with a sense of her wrongs. We forbear to aggravate our resentment by dwelling upon the various degrading opinions that have successively prevailed in reference to her nature and destination; or upon the policy consequently adopted, the world over, and up to the present time, in relation to the development and cultivation of her mind. We will not number and fathom the institutions, venerable for their antiquity, and munificently endowed, established for the education of men; nor advert to the frequency and care with which similar institutions are rising around us on every hand; and then place in mortifying contrast the utter destitution of such establishments for females, and the vast effort with which their semblance even has, in a few instances, been secured; — we will not say that though the claims of man are paramount, woman has yet her claims — that her nature is not all, unlike his own, nor the sphere she occupies at an infinite remove from his; — we will not dwell upon these soul-stirring truths, — but raise our hands and our hearts to heaven, that, through the tender mercy of our God, the day-spring from on high hath visited us. We see its glad tokens in the slow but certain change pervading the public mind, in reference to female education. Ladies, the gifted and the good, have plead our cause, and they have not plead in vain. Gentlemen, with their characteristic generosity of heart and liberality of mind, are coming nobly forward to our rescue, with a chivalry truly worthy of their nature. In this let us see, and with the profoundest gratitude acknowledge, the hand of God. Let his goodness lead us to sincere repentance, and, in humble reliance upon Him, let us gird ourselves to coöperate in so exalted a work.

The sphere of woman is, at the present day, far more extended than at any previous period of the world's history. In proportion as her talents are appreciated, she comes to be placed in stations of trust. To the missionary enterprise, and the example of our beloved Mrs. Judson, are we much indebted for the proof of what woman *might* do. Amid the solitude and gloom of heathenism, there was no room for narrow jealousy, lest woman should tread too closely upon the steps of her husband; there her energies were demanded, and they were at hand. The experiment was made, and the astonishing result brought to light, that, through the instrumentality of woman, the soul shrouded in Egyptian night might be disenthralled, and brought gloriously forth to behold the Sun of Righteousness. Woman is no longer limited in her range to the sequestered walks of private life. To wield the implements of Ceres, and practise the slender arts of Minerva — to soothe the tumultuous passions of her lord, and inspire his soul with calm and holy thought — to guide the footsteps of her infant train in the paths of virtue — to watch beside the couch of sickness, and smooth the pillow of death; — these, though they constitute the scenes in which she most loves to mingle, are not her only enjoyments. Hers is the task to rear the tender thought, to guide the wayward fancy, and to form the soul, from dawning infancy, to blushing woman-hood ; — and hers, to wield the pen, transferring thoughts that burn, and clothing truth in her own native drapery ; — to trace the avenues to human misery, fathom its depths, and, like mercy's angel, bring relief ; — to burst the bands of kindred, and with dauntless courage bear o'er the billowy deep the olive-branch of peace.

Such is the destiny of woman, and such the spheres for which she must be fitted by education. The work is a great one, but in proportion to its magnitude must be our schemes for its accomplishment. If the education of young men requires large and expensive establishments of halls, cabinets, libraries, apparatus and a host of professors, something not totally unlike to this should be provided for females. We cannot learn, neither can we teach, by a sort of magic peculiar to ourselves ; give us the facilities for education enjoyed by the other sex, and we shall at least be able to try what are the capabilities of woman.

————

FEMALE EDUCATION.

> " What of lovely grows on wisdom's tree,
> Fair sister, is, or should be, plucked by thee ;
> Not feigned arts to please and charm the eyes,
> But such as grace the daughters of the skies."

Perhaps no sentiment is more common, whether expressed in words or in the less equivocal language of action, than that an elaborate education is lost upon a lady, unless she is led to assume the occupation of a teacher, or is called to frequent the walks of refined and fashionable life. Now I think it abun-

dantly susceptible of proof, that whether woman is
regarded in the relation she sustains to her *Creator*,
as an intelligent, moral being; to *man*, as his companion and helper; to *herself*, as possessing equally
with man the sacred and inalienable right of pursuing
her own happiness; to the *present generation*, as con-
trolling the intellectual tastes, and graduating the
moral tone of society; to the *coming generation*, as
absolutely determining its character, and moulding it
at her will; a *thorough, extensive*, and highly finished
education, is of the first importance.   For how can
she worship God in a manner suited to his character,
unless she have definite and impressive views of that
character?   How adore him with elevated affections,
unless she is able to apprehend and distinctly to contemplate his attributes?   How obey his laws, unless
she is able to discover those laws?   That God does
consider such a knowledge of himself, and of the
principles of his administration, essential to our highest happiness, is evident from the ample means he
has provided for the attainment of this end.   No less
than three incomparable volumes has he thrown open
before us; the first, his *universe of matter* and of *mind*;
the second, the *system* of *his natural* and *moral* government, or his course of Providence; the third, his
written Word.   Now the whole system of education
properly consists in the study of these volumes, for
the purpose for which they were designed, and to
which they are most admirably adapted, that of raising the human soul to the highest point of elevation
of which its nature is susceptible.   The sciences,
respectively considered, are so many chapters upon

the perfection of Deity, calling forth the profoundest admiration and homage of our hearts. They are so many emanations from the Divine Mind, no one of which, if legitimately pursued, does not lead us back to its source. Shall it be said, then, that woman need not be initiated into the mysteries of science? God has opened the volume before her, and who will presume to withhold from her the means of deciphering the awful page?

To deny that woman should enjoy the perfecting hand of education, when considered as the companion and helper of man, would imply such a derogation of *his* character, as we think he would feel no ambition to claim. The very idea of companionship, though it may admit of certain diversities, implies an essential equality. It implies that the character, in its leading features, be graduated by the same scale. Indeed it is the simplest dictate of reason, that intelligence has no companionship with stupidity, refinement with rudeness, or a richly cultivated and energetic mind, with barrenness and imbecility. Personal beauty, indeed, has powerful charms, "so God ordains," but it is only when combined with corresponding beauty of intellect and of sentiment, that it can stand the ordeal of long and intimate acquaintance.

As an individual, permitted by right, and bound by duty, to pursue her own happiness, woman should bestow the highest possible attention upon the development of her mind. The very element of happiness consists in the exercise of the several faculties with which our Creator has endowed us. Is it for

our happiness, then, that these faculties should be
in perpetual embryo, and never be brought into
contact with those objects which are calculated to
awaken them into activity? O, how many a burning sentiment, how many a heavenly aspiration, has
been quenched in the unfathomed mine, as diamonds
destined never to imbibe the solar ray !

But the most exalted element of woman's happiness lies in her power of communicating happiness
to others. Deprive her of this privilege, and you
make her miserable indeed. How cruel, then to rob
her of the chief and only certain means of securing
this blessedness, — a highly wrought and beautifully
polished soul.

It is allowed that the whole face of society receives
its impress from the character of woman ; and that
it is her peculiar province to form the rising mind.
In this point of view, regarding society as it is, and
as it is to be, the subject of female education addresses
itself most powerfully both to the philanthropist and
to the statesman. It cannot be denied that mankind are not more creatures of *imitation* than of *as-
similation*. We are disposed not only to act like
those around us, but to become like those around
us. The most superficial observer cannot have failed
to notice this fact in relation to himself, at a period
of life however advanced, and under circumstances
comparatively unfavorable. How powerful, then,
must be the effect of this principle upon the plastic
infant mind, under the fostering hand of that being
around whom all the fibres of the heart are entwined.
The infant will imbibe the nicest shades of its mo-

ther's character; her thoughts, her feelings, her tastes, her attitudes and her idioms, infuse themselves with a strange subtlety into its soul, and become essential elements of its very constitution. How immense then the power that is vested in the hand of woman! No matter what be her condition; it is enough that she is a woman, that no pains be spared to render her virtuous, intelligent, and accomplished.

You will observe, my dear young ladies, that I have presented the subject of female education with exclusive reference to the practical duties of life; and it is with such a reference that I think it should always be regarded. Any study which is not in some way calculated to enable us more perfectly to answer the end designed by the Creator in our formation, should be at once rejected as not only useless, but criminal; inasmuch as it engrosses a portion of our energies and our time, both sacred deposites committed to us as stewards, and which we are at liberty to appropriate only at the direction of our Master. We should be cautious however, not to be hasty in pronouncing any species of discipline useless; it may have bearings which are not at once perceived. It is not uncommon to hear the ornamental branches of education decried *en masse*; and yet they exert a powerful, though subtle influence upon the mind, which cannot be fully traced by any other than a philosophic eye. Their general tendency is happily recognised in the language of the poet, —

> " These polished arts have humanized mankind,
> Softened the rude, and calmed the boisterous mind."

Drawing, music, and poetry, are preëminently calculated to refine the taste, and to afford pleasure of the
most innocent and ennobling kind ; and even the less
exalted arts of fancy needle-work, and trifling parlor
decorations, have their beneficial effects in cultivating
a chastened elegance of taste, and a practical sense
of the beautiful.   The only danger in relation to the
pursuit of these branches is, lest we appropriate to
them an undue share of our attention.   Although
they have a value, they must give place, in point of
utility, to many other claims ; and it becomes our
duty scrupulously to inquire for what pursuits Providence has especially designed us as individuals, and
to shape our education accordingly.   We should
never forget, however, that as a sex, it is our peculiar province to please.   This is unquestionably one
design of the Creator, in relation to ourselves, and
should not be overlooked by us.   We should place
an appropriate value upon our personal attractions,
and should be careful that in our attire we do not
degrade that beautiful fabric which the Deity thought
fit to create as the investment of the soul.   The art
of conversing with vivacity and elegance is of great
value to a lady, as it enables her not only to please,
but to benefit others by the acceptable communication of her thoughts.   There is also what may be
styled the " poetry of action," a certain gracefulness
of address, which possesses irresistible charms.   These
things are not matters of caprice ; they have their
foundation in the constitution of the human mind,
and should not be regarded as beneath our notice.
I am the more particular in relation to these points

of embellishment, as I am aware that the genius of some of our best literary institutions tends to overlook them, and am unwilling that scientific and literary attainment in ladies, should be brought into discredit, by being generally found associated with inattention to personal appearance, uncouthness of manners, and a neglect of the elegant and graceful.

FEMALE EDUCATION.

" Go, sister, and bless mankind
With wisdom, grace, and household goods combined."

It is a subject of regret that many who have appeared well while at school, and have perhaps acquired distinction in their classes, when entering the sphere of domestic life, seem almost to forfeit their claim to intelligence, and become dull and uninteresting companions. This may be owing in part to the force of circumstances, but chiefly, I am persuaded, to wrong intellectual habits. They have been taught science at school, in an abstract form, and rather as matter of theory than practice. From the nature of the case, this is unavoidable. It is true, experiments will be made, and examples supplied, while at school, to render the pupil master of his subject ; but these must of necessity be few. In the common occurrences and ordinary intercourse of life, experiments are continually going on, and phenomena constantly exhibited, which may be of immense profit to the observing mind. What I wish particularly to recommend is, that these phenomena be carefully noticed, and their relation to their respective sciences accurately traced. Should a young lady find herself unable, in any instance, successfully to prosecute her reflections, let her *by no means* relinquish the subject, but lay it by, both in her memory and in her common-place book, as a question for future solution, and in her subsequent intercourse with men and books, let her watch for an opportunity of obtaining the information desired. By this means she will come to understand fully and practically those principles with which she was before but partially acquainted; and the knowledge thus obtained will possess for her a double value from the fact that it will have been acquired by her own patient induction and persevering effort.

The second thing which I would notice, is the importance of *systematic thinking*, in opposition to that state of passive reverie, in which so many indulge. Young ladies are peculiarly apt to be faulty here. Owing to the quiet retirement of domestic life, and the few striking incidents that are likely there to occur, they are in danger of losing their elasticity, and of becoming the victims of mental indolence. Urged forward by no irresistible impulse, and wanting resolution to impose upon themselves the most salutary tasks, they allow their thoughts to succeed each other by the force of casual associations, till they lose all control of the operations of their minds. It is then you hear them complaining of the insipidity of human life, and driven to the dire necessity of seeking amusement, you behold them escaping to the regions of fiction, to beguile the tedium of their existence.

Such are the inebriates which grace many a parlor.
Disgusted themselves with everything around them,
they cannot fail soon to become, in their turn, objects of disgust. That all these evil results may be
legitimately traced to lax habits of thought, and the
want of suitable mental discipline, constantly kept
up, I have not a doubt. Beware then, young ladies,
of considering your education finished, when you
leave school. You may have received a liberal course
of instruction, and may possess the most satisfactory
testimonials of your scholarship, but believe me, if a
right course be not pursued, subsequent to your
graduating at school, your attainments will be as the
early dew. It is a truth which many a tender father
has learned to the anguish of his heart, that the re-
spectability and usefulness of his daughter, in the
sequel of her life, are not necessarily in proportion to
the expense bestowed upon her education, nor even
to her progress while at school. Knowledge is not,
as some seem to have supposed, a sure and permanent fund ; moth and rust may corrupt it, or it may
take to itself wings and fly away. It is indeed capi-
tal which may be so invested as to yield a hundred-
fold, or it may be so squandered as to leave its former
possessor a bankrupt and vagabond. Employ then
every possible means to sustain the activity of your
minds. I would not have you indulge in a disputa-
tious spirit, but I *would* have you cherish most as-
siduously a habit of close, persevering investigation.
Truth is the philosopher's stone, and though some
truths may be of less importance than others, they
have each a *value*, which, if duly appreciated, will

prove a sovereign antidote to that mental sloth, which so often nearly annihilates the soul.

As an important means of accomplishing what is desirable in relation to the progress of your minds, I would recommend that you endeavor to keep pace with literature as it rises. Interest yourself in new publications. If you cannot obtain them all, you can at least obtain a *Review* of the most valuable. The North American Review will present you much of the literature of our own country, and the Edinburg, with that of England. The Annals of Education you will find invaluable. The Quarterly Observer and Repository, the Religious Magazine, and the Quarterly Christian Spectator, contain much that is rich of religious literature. Our best missionary journals are familiar to all; of these I need not speak. Do not be parsimonious in your appropriations for such periodicals, as well as for standard works for your libraries. It is one of the happiest features in the improvements of the present day, that we have learned to dress as gracefully as heretofore, at much less expense. By a little ingenuity, considerable improvements may still be made in this department. The article of diet presents another item of expenditure, in which *very much* may be saved. I have not yet adopted the Graham system, but am persuaded most of us would think with greater effect, were our regimen more simple. I do hope the period is advancing, when the all-absorbing inquiry will not be, what shall we eat, and what shall we drink, and wherewithal shall we be clothed, but when our aim shall be steadily fixed upon that which is chiefly worthy the dignity of our nature, an acquaintance with ourselves, and with the Deity.

But perhaps the most effectual stimulus to mental activity, is to be found in the exercise of practical benevolence. In order to the accomplishment of any object, an adequate motive must be supplied ; and I doubt whether the consideration of personal advantage, great as this may be, will generally be found of sufficient power, to rouse the sluggish energies of the soul. But the hope of doing good to others, of relieving the wretchedness of woe, of imparting gladness to the disconsolate heart, of dispensing joy, as the pure light of heaven throughout all the region of our influence, furnishes an incentive the most powerful that can possibly be conceived. It not only prompts to the invention of numerous expedients, by which the faculties of the mind are called into salutary exercise, but it conduces greatly to that healthful state of moral feeling, which is the grand renovator of the intellect. There is not a virtue which it does not cherish. It is the soil whence springs everything excellent and lovely in the female character.

But do not suppose that your charities are to be bestowed entirely, or chiefly, abroad ; this would be to fall into a fatal mistake. Let not the *woman* be lost in the scholar, or even in the philanthropist ; — *home* is your own appropriate sphere. If you are wanting in your duties *there*, you strike a deadly blow at those very objects which you would so zealously support. Strive, then, to be a pattern of all that is lovely in your own domestic circle — here lies our praise, here our true honor. Finally, my dear

23*

young friends, if you would be *perfect, wanting in nothing,* let me beseech you to study most attentively, most prayerfully, and with the deepest humility of heart, the *oracles of divine truth.* Take them emphatically as the man of your counsel, and adhere implicitly to the directions therein given. I can wish you no greater blessing than that you may grow in grace, and in the knowledge of our Lord Jesus Christ.

DIGNITY OF THE SABBATH SCHOOL ENTERPRISE.

In forming the scheme of universal nature, it evidently constituted no part of the design of the great Architect to secure for his sentient creatures an exemption from labor; on the contrary, having made the very element of happiness to consist in action, he appears to have taken special care to furnish every order of his creatures with appropriate occasions for activity. Hence we observe him studiously avoiding to effect by his own immediate agency, whatever is within the compass of their capacities.

The benevolence, no less than the wisdom of his economy, can never be sufficiently admired : it presents a delightful order of natural relations and dependencies, specially adapted to the nature of man as an intellectual and moral being. It affords ample exercise to his noblest faculties; to his intellect and his conscience in the discovery of his various relations, and of the duty arising out of these relations; to his affections in yielding a voluntary compliance with the laws of his Creator thus discovered. **No** other scheme of things can be conceived, so admirably adapted to fit him for his high destiny. By this, he is permitted to become at once a co-worker with God; is brought within the immediate sphere of his personal influence, and taught habitually to recognise his superintendence and authority.

We have regarded the plan of Jehovah's operations as a *system* made up of various parts, and as, in the visible church of the Redeemer, "the eye cannot say unto the hand, I have no need of thee; nor, again, the head to the feet, I have no need of you;" so of the several departments of God's universal scheme. But although the relation in which we stand to our Creator renders it our duty to submit implicitly to his will in reference to the sphere of our own exertions, we cannot be insensible to the fact, that certain departments of action are in themselves more elevated and more desirable than others. It is the comparative dignity and advantages of the Sabbath school enterprise which we are now to consider.

Of all avocations, the formation of human character must be the most elevated and responsible. It is a work, too, accomplished by no single instrumentality. The mother commences even before the period when she lulls her infant to repose by her cradlesong; inanimate nature assumes no small share of the task; the various grades of schools, from the infant and primary to the collegiate and professional, perform their part; and promiscuous society, and a course of events seemingly fortuitous, greatly modify the result.

But what is the effect of these various modes of discipline upon the great object of interest, the human soul? We ask not what they might be, what they *should* be, but what they *are?* The mother, though she knows indeed that her infant charge is a complex existence, made up of matter and spirit, the former of which is but the temporary tenement of the latter, bestows nevertheless her chief solicitude upon its physical necessities. Too often, alas! does she seem insensible to the fact, that a germ of priceless worth is striking its roots in the soil of her own influence. To secure for her little one suitable regimen, neat and becoming attire, and general correctness of habit, constitutes the main end of her endeavor. He goes forth from her arms to gaze upon and admire a multitude of objects, scattered in profusion over the face of nature. He learns their properties, relations and susceptibilities, and may, perchance, be led to recognise in these a designing Mind or a forming Hand. But whose task is it to direct its infant apprehension to retain this idea as its very life, and to acknowledge and adore that Being as the Great Supreme? The mother cannot do it; her engagements are too numerous and too pressing, as she supposes, to allow her to undertake the duty, and she soon devolves upon the teacher all her care for the education of her offspring.

But does the teacher assume this responsibility? No; he undertakes indeed to cultivate the mind of his pupil, and to teach him letters; but the duty of training the conscience and the affections is with him a secondary object. Nor is it of any avail to rely upon the influence of higher institutions for the inculcation of moral principle. A profound knowledge of the sciences and the acquisition of intellectual power, is the great desideratum of the schools. Upon whom, then, shall it devolve to train the soul for heaven? Do you reply, upon the minister? I answer, the minister has but very partial access to the individual until his habits have become confirmed, and the ductility of his mind is lost. It is upon the Sabbath school teacher, it is upon yourselves, that this solemn duty must rest. The mind, as affected by other influences, with regard to the great purpose of existence, becomes like the mighty elements of nature, roaming, boisterous and wild. A presiding genius must tame its ferocity, and turn to their proper account its mighty energies. Here lies the sublimity of your province. The assiduity of the mother, the toil of the father, the efforts of the teacher, the silent lessons of nature, and the dispensations of a guardian Providence, are all placed at your disposal. What application will you make of this accumulation of material? Will you erect a fabric worthy to become the temple of the Holy Ghost, complete from its foundation to the topmost stone? Or will you allow all these advantages to be scattered to the heedless winds, or combined by an evil genius to form " vessels of wrath fitted for destruction "?

The Sabbath school teacher sustains an important relation, not only to the church, but to the world; not only to individual, but to human destiny. It is to him especially that the church is looking, to form the character of her sons; that they may be grounded in the truth, and not, like children, tossed to and

fro by every wind of doctrine; that they may be men
of consistent piety, whose readiness to every good
word and work has been confirmed into an unalterable
habit, and not those whose zeal and devotion are fitful
and fluctuating; men whose principles rest upon a
clear understanding of the oracles of eternal truth,
not upon vague and uncertain notions contracted
from the atmosphere of human opinions.

Nor are his efforts scarcely less necessary to the
well being of civil society. Learning, unless combined with religion, is no safeguard to national prosperity. The fear of the Lord is the beginning of
wisdom, not only with respect to individuals, but to
communities. To form a people for Jehovah, and
nations whose God shall be the Lord, is the province
of the Sabbath school.

But, regarding the individual interests alone of
those who are the immediate objects of his labor, the
responsibilities of the Sabbath school teacher are beyond computation. The condition of their being,
not only in the present life, but through unceasing
ages, is, to a great degree, subject to his decision.
The consequences of the course which he pursues
toward his pupil, will be developing and augmenting
in a fearful ratio to all eternity. How vastly important, then, that his best energies be summoned to a
work so elevated, so responsible!

But notwithstanding the greatness of the work,
the Sabbath school enterprise possesses many and
important advantages over every other system of instruction. The sacred stillness of the Sabbath, with
all its hallowed associations, — the solemn assem-

bling of those who are ordinarily so full of merriment and glee, to receive lessons of heavenly wisdom, — the serious, but gentle, winning carriage of the teachers, appearing like angels of mercy pointing the wanderer to the skies, are circumstances extremely favorable to religious impression.

Here, too, the pupil may be addressed with the most affectionate familiarity; the obstacles to his conversion may be successfully sought out, and such instructions imparted as are specially adapted to his necessities.   Nor are these lessons merely occasional, but occurring in a series from week to week, afford peculiar facilities for leading the mind along from step to step to the great end to be attained.   The affectionate, confiding disposition of children, gives a teacher that influence over them which enables him to mould their characters almost at will.   This is peculiarly seen in respect to the Sabbath school teacher; for notwithstanding our natural aversion to holiness, we feel a mysterious attachment for those who are accustomed to converse with us tenderly upon the interests of the soul.

The circumstance, too, of passing from the Sabbath school, as is usually the case, into the sanctuary for public worship, is one of great importance.   Here the lessons received in school are sanctioned and enforced from the sacred desk, and by this means held so long before the mind, as almost necessarily to leave a permanent impression.

Under all these advantages, with what ardor should the Sabbath school teacher enter upon his work! How glorious thus to labor for the best interests of

our pupils, for the world of mankind in general, for
the support and upbuilding of the Church of the
Redeemer!

QUALIFICATIONS OF THE SABBATH SCHOOL TEACHER.

The Sabbath school teacher should be deeply sensible of the work in which he is engaged, and of the
immense responsibilities connected with it.   This
may be regarded as his first qualification, inasmuch
as it almost necessarily secures every other.   It will
inspire him with an ardor of pursuit which nothing
can abate, and enlist the best energies of his mind
in devising means for the accomplishment of his object, and in carrying those means into operation.

But, to specify more particularly, the Sabbath school
teacher should possess a systematic and accurate
knowledge of the volume of divine inspiration.   His
leading object is to form the character of his pupils upon the model of the Sacred Scriptures, and to
put them in possession of such principles as shall secure their progress in christian attainment, and their
final admission to heaven.   Now there are no means
adequate to this result other than the system of Bible truth.   If, then, the teacher would accomplish
his object, he must be intimately acquainted with his
Bible.   He should not only have a correct understanding of many important passages, but a connected, complete view of the whole volume.   There is
no commentary upon sacred writ so valuable, as that
which is found *in* the Bible itself; and no means

of discovering the true sense of Scripture, so effectual as that which is derived from a correct apprehension of the general scope of the discourse.

The teacher should also possess a knowledge of the manners and customs, institutions and spirit of the times in which the Scriptures were written, with the natural scenery and ordinary objects and events from which the sacred writers have drawn their illustrations. He should understand the acknowledged principles of interpretation, and, if possible, the original languages in which the Scriptures were written. These advantages will give him a confidence and satisfaction respecting the correctness of the views he advances, which will materially contribute to his success. It is of vast importance that the Scriptures be taught systematically, that children be able to read them understandingly for themselves. They should know upon what basis their authenticity rests, and upon what principle to harmonize passages apparently incompatible. It is only in this way that they will ever assume that independence of investigation, which, as it is indispensable to high attainments in anything else, is no less so in piety.

The superficial knowledge of the Bible which is generally possessed, is matter of astonishment and shame. We have one small volume alone, which we acknowledge to be a revelation from God, and yet how few professing Christians are able to give anything like a correct analysis of its contents! The reason is obvious. There has been a radical defect in the manner in which it has been taught. The professed ministers of the Gospel have, perhaps, done what might be expected of them in this repect; but they have not those facilities which the Sabbath school affords for imparting a comprehensive, and at the same time accurate acquaintance with the sacred text. But this object should be effected by some means; it *must* be effected, before we can hope to see the church exhibit that perfection of beauty, and its members that symmetry of character, which should be the highest object of desire to every Christian.

Let not the teacher complain that we are placing our aim altogether too high, that it is in vain to hope to make divines of children. He should beware of setting too low an estimate upon the capabilities of his pupils, and of becoming discouraged by their stupidity or inattention. Grant that they do not seem to apprehend very readily, and that they do not manifest that interest which is desirable; he should do all in his power, indeed, to obviate these difficulties; but let him, by no means, on this account, withhold from them his best instructions. He will need to repeat them many times; but let him feel assured, that if he pursues his duty with a right spirit, his labors will not be lost. If he persevere in an energetic and elevated course of instruction, his pupils will be found to possess, not only a large amount of valuable knowledge, but a tolerably correct and consistent system of christian truth, their stupidity and inattention notwithstanding.

THE present condition of our being is evidently not the happiest of which we might conceive. However perfect it might be regarded in relation to another state of existence, it presents in itself a picture of confusion and sorrow, but partially relieved by slight intervals of gladness and repose. The sources of this unhappiness are chiefly to be sought in our ignorance of the laws of our being, and the want of harmony between our moral feelings and these laws so far as discovered. It is the province of education to reduce these jarring elements to order, and change this wilderness of tears to the garden of hope. This result must be effected, instrumentally, by the study of truth, and the development and right regulation of the several faculties of the soul.

The various subjects of our studies may be regarded as falling under three departments: the nature of material things, their various relation to each other, and to human condition; the nature, susceptibilities and relations of human intellect; and the character and prerogatives of Deity. Of these the former engrosses a large and disproportionate share of our attention, and of itself affords such numberless varieties, and a range so wide, as, without the aid of philosophy, utterly to baffle human apprehension. The other departments may seem less extended, because more subtle in their nature, and therefore veiled from ordinary observation; yet in truth they present a scope even more ample, and are in themselves so intricate and profound as to tax the utmost power of thought.

The great key to all science is classification. Without it human knowledge were as good as at an end. It is the principle of generic resemblances amid infinite individual variety, pervading every department of being, which constitutes the mystic thread, unfolding nature's labyrinth, and subjecting universal truth to the control of man. On entering a field of observation like that before us, it is of the first importance that our inquiries be skilfully conducted. As we trace the progress of science thus far, from the moment man first looked forth upon the vast expanse of human existence to the present time, at which we scarce find a fresh field for the scientific adventurer, we cannot but admire the prodigious amount of intellectual labor which has actually been accomplished. We find in our possession the spoils of ages ; and it is ours, if not unworthy of our heritage, to add yet other trophies to their number, to carry forward and perfect investigations thus far pursued, to add truth to truth, and in our turn transmit to posterity, with accumulated value, the boon received from those who have gone before us. This is the highest department now open to human intellect ; and though we may not hope to enter at once upon it, we should beware of regarding it as beyond our ultimate range. With the grand lever of philosophy in his hand, the weakest need not despair.

As teachers of youth, however, our sphere is somewhat humbler. We cannot hope to lead our pupils to the temple of fame ; we can only lay the foundation for eminence in a thoroughly-disciplined and well-developed mind. Farther than this depends

alone upon themselves. It is ours to lead them
safely through the mazes of science, from its simplest
principles as far as possible toward the summit of its
present attainment; and to do this by such means as
will secure the greatest energy and scope of mind,
the most just and cultivated literary taste, and the
most deeply-laid religious sentiment. This is no
easy task. To the careless and indolent, everything
is found ready to his hand ; the leading laws of the
various sciences are all detected, verified and classed,
so that he has but to con the page, and his work is
done. This course is fatal to vigor and depth of
mind, and almost equally so to sound learning. The
only true means of securing the end of study, is to
lead the pupil through essentially the same process
by which the several truths were originally arrived
at. After this is done, and the principle obtained
and thoroughly examined, let him have the satisfaction to know that he has trodden the same path, and
arrived at the same result, the great had done before
him. This process may be successfully pursued in
almost every study, by a skilful and assiduous teacher.
Its nature is happily illustrated by the process of acquiring language. Our knowledge of the meaning
of words in our native tongue, is inevitably acquired
almost entirely by laborious induction from a series
of careful comparisons. The mode of acquiring a
foreign tongue is essentially the same. Were we to
depend in either exclusively upon the aid of a dictionary, our knowledge of the language must be
found entirely defective. It is the same in rhetoric.
The only effectual means of obtaining any practical

knowledge of its principles, is by that same observation of the various effects upon the mind of the several qualities of writing, by which original authors on this subject prepared their works. The principle is equally true in reference to arithmetic, intellectual philosophy, the several branches of natural science, and to theology. In pursuing the study of intellectual philosophy, for example, we should place before the learner facts in relation to mind, and direct him to draw his own inference. We may then show him that the same principle is recognised by Bacon, by Brown, and by Stewart. By this process of discovery his own faculties have received a salutary exercise, he is made to possess a consciousness of his powers, and encouraged to prosecute his inquiries. Now let the order have been inverted; let the pupil have been allowed to read the principle in some scientific work, and perhaps to have read also its proof, or the data upon which it rests, he may be, in some sense, acquainted with the principle in question; but, instead of being so incorporated with his very intellections as to constitute a part of his mind itself, his knowledge will be superficial and but feebly apprehended, and will, most probably, prove of very little account by way of application to practice. The whole course of a scholar's education should be that of accurate observation, analysis and classification. He should aim at the attainment of general principles, in everything; and that, too, by the only legitimate process, a careful induction. When this is done, he will be able to apply these principles to the numberless details of common life, with the skill and certainty of a philosopher.

The basis of education being thus laid, there is no degree of intellectual attainment which the scholar may not hope. The works of others are analyzed with a giant power, and whatsoever is new or useful gleaned at a glance. The whole range of science lies at his control, and he may drink to his heart's content at the fountain of knowledge.

The next thing to be secured is a correct and cultivated literary taste. Of this the principles are deeply laid; they are interwoven with the finest fibres of the soul, and should be skilfully cultivated from early childhood. Of such cultivation alone, that intuitive sense which judges instinctively of literary merit is the result. Language is the organ of sentiment and of imagination, as well as of reason. It is designed naturally and faithfully to transmit these incorporeal essences from mind to mind. If true to its design, the soul enjoys the harmony; if false, it feels the discord. A knowledge of the human passions, and of their appropriate language, is an essential element of literary taste.

The ability to seize the *beau ideal* in every department of literary effort, and to judge of every performance with reference to it, can be acquired only by repeated observation and comparison of the various standard works, under their several heads. Here nature must be studied, not only in her corporeal, but in her abstract forms; not only in her exact imitations, but in the high-wrought pictures of the orator and poet. Drawings of human character, upon the same principle of abstract beauty, afford lessons of the deepest interest; and history, in a master's hand,

holds up the grand drama of human life in the same
enchanting mirror.   Such models combine harmony
and truth in their greatest perfection.   They arouse
the sensibility, and awaken a quick perception of the
beautiful, wherever found.   Like the divine pencil of
Correggio, they call up new powers in the human
soul, and invest universal nature with corresponding
charms.

But it is not to be supposed that, when these points
are secured, the great end of education is attained.
The first evil from which the miseries of our condition were supposed to arise, has indeed found its
remedy ; but the latter and more important point remains to be gained.   There have been many who
have gone thus far, and died as they lived, strangers
to peace.   Indeed, nothing is more dangerous than
such an intellectual elevation, where the moral feelings have been neglected.   A knowledge of the laws
of God furnishes the highest facilities for a holy life,
and the most powerful incentives to it ; but if the religious impressions conveyed by the first discovered
truths are suffered to pass unregarded, the avenue
to the fountain of wisdom becomes more obscure and
difficult, till at length obstructed by impervious night.
For this reason the greatest care should be taken,
during the earliest steps in the intellectual education, that every law of nature, when presented to the
mind, be rightly interpreted as delineating some feature of the Deity, and involving a corresponding
modification of our relations and duty to him.   This
process should be constantly pursued through the
whole course of education.   The providences of God,

as recorded upon the pages of history, both sacred and profane, as passing under our own observation, or subject to personal experience, should all teach us the attributes of our Creator, and the laws under which he has placed us. It is true we may find all the results of these observations, so far as they are correct, embodied in the Word of God; but if inattentive to the voice of nature, we may never trace them there, and shall be sure never to feel their full force until they are corroborated as matter of experience, or as the result of rational deduction.

The work of education, then, is an arduous and an elevated task. If its importance be graduated by the change produced upon its subject, this truth will abundantly appear. These effects have been compared to those of the statuary's art upon the shapeless marble, from which the magic of his chisel brings the breathing form. But the comparison utterly fails fully to set forth the truth it so happily illustrates. The material upon which the educator operates defies comparison, and the results of his labor, if skilfully and faithfully directed, infinitely surpass the divinest products of the artist's skill. The force of education Philip felt, when he says, in committing his only son to the charge of Aristotle, "You will hereafter be his father more truly than I myself."

If the importance of education be graduated by its effects upon man's entire condition, the position is equally obvious. To him who knows and loves the laws of his Creator nature is no longer at variance. The divine administration no longer appears veiled in obscurity, but pervaded by one great principle of moral rectitude, running through all time, and entering the veil of eternity. To him the present state of human existence is viewed in its true light, as affording an arena for a moral action, and a school for the formation of moral character, admirably adapted to its end. To him the ills of life are but harbingers of joy, pointing to the bright vista of immortality.

MISS HAZELTINE'S LAST COMMUNICATION TO THE ACTING MEMBERS OF THE ASSOCIATION OF THE NEW HAMPTON FEMALE SEMINARY, WHILE CORRESPONDING SECRETARY.

In attempting to present a few thoughts to the members of the beloved Association which it is my privilege once more to report, I shall be credited, I doubt not, when I say, that the question on which my choice of a theme has turned, is simply this : — In what point is the little influence I may hope to exert by this effort most needed? On surveying the whole field of female action and influence, considering the capabilities of woman, and the means at present in operation for their development and application, her important rank in society, and her responsibilities and hopes as a moral and accountable being, I have felt deeply impressed with the belief that *nothing is so much needed, in order to promote the usefulness and the welfare of woman, as* PRINCIPLE. I shall, therefore, offer a few remarks upon this subject, and shall consider it, *first*, as opposed to passiveness or indecision ; *secondly*, to habit ; *thirdly*, to prejudice and caprice ;

fourthly, to policy or artifice; *fifthly*, to dishonesty and impiety.

PRINCIPLE, as opposed to *passiveness*, implies a definite and fixed standard of the just and fit. It is that property which marks the uniform and efficient. It is that which commands our involuntary deference and respect, and which, in its sphere, secures our confidence. In its analysis it has many points of coincidence with taste, as that term' is defined in works of rhetoric. Like taste, its foundation is laid in the structure of the human mind. Like taste, it is built on the experience of emotions, if not of the beautiful and its opposite, certainly of the fit and becoming. Like taste, it is cultivated by attention to these emotions, by the study of models, and by habits of generalization, and like taste, becomes so wrought into our natures as to assume the character of an instinct, and to put forth its exercises with the same promptitude and unerring certainty.

In reference to the points above named, we have compared principle to taste. It may also, in certain particulars, be compared to conscience. Like conscience, the more promptly its dictates are obeyed, the more acute becomes its power of discrimination; and like conscience, its voice is silenced when habitually unheeded. Like conscience, too, it has its scourge. No one ever indulges knowingly in a breach of propriety, without feeling its lashes. In many it is even more powerful than conscience. It tortures at the midnight hour that mind in which conscience profoundly slumbers. Not that it should have this ascendancy; this we are far from admitting; we are only concerned to prove that principle, as opposed to passiveness, is not an element of character arbitrary and indefinable, but founded in nature, distinctly marked, and sustaining a most important relation to the multiplied interests of man.

From what I have said, my readers will naturally have associated *principle*, as defined and illustrated above, with the well-known phrase *decision of character*. To this I have no objection. It differs from the trait implied in that term only as an antecedent from its consequent, as a cause from its effect, as a fountain from the stream that flows from it.

The pernicious effects of indecision, and the pain it causes its subject, we have most of us, probably, too often experienced. They surely need not, therefore, be enumerated and developed here. To feel ourselves floating at the will of the popular tide, or drawn like a comet out of our course, first by the influence of this individual, and then of that; to be torn asunder in our own minds, by opposing resolutions, forever vacillating and irresolute, is neither very flattering to our self-esteem, nor conducive to our comfort. Such a habit takes from us all chance for success in the pursuit of any valuable end, and entirely palsies our power of eminent usefulness to others.

PRINCIPLE, as opposed to *habit*, implies a just perception of the relations of things, whether fixed or variable, and the power of adapting one's course of action to these relations. It is that which distinguishes the science of the mechanician from the dexterity of the artisan, or the philosophic skill of the enlightened physician from the quackery of the empirist. In presuming to set aside habit as a governing principle of human action, I may seem to be opposing the popular sentiment. We have been so often harangued upon the power of habit, and moralists, even, have so often philosophized upon it with much simplicity and justice, and assigned it so prominent a place in the composition of human character, that we may have come to receive, almost without scruple, the dogma, that "man is but a bundle of habits." We readily admit the vast power of habit; we admit the whole doctrine of habit as developed in a late and deservedly popular work on moral science. We believe it cannot be spoken against as an element entering into the economy of the human constitution, and into that of God's scheme of moral government. But we reject it, we deprecate it as a governing principle. It may be turned to the best account, as a promoter of happiness, when controlled by intelligence and wisdom; but, as a master principle, it is an arbitrary tyrant. The actions which it prompts are essentially mechanical; they have none of the features which constitute the glory of humanity; they bear the impress neither of freedom nor of consciousness.

That system of education, therefore, which aims merely or chiefly at establishing habits, we think fundamentally defective. It will not stand the test of varied experiment. It is true, character would be but poorly established were no habits formed; but these are not enough. The mind trained simply to habits, is destitute of flexibility. It may tread well in the beaten path, but vary its course, however little, and all is amazement. Let character, then, be consolidated by virtuous habit; but let it be vitalized and controlled by principle.

PRINCIPLE, as opposed to *prejudice* and *caprice*, is an exact regard to evidence and to reason. On this head very little need be said. There is scarcely any one who does not readily acknowledge the claims of principle, when viewed in this relation. Every one would feel it an insult to his understanding to suppose him prejudiced or capricious. I do not say that all are free from the influence of prejudice; I am far from believing it; nor that some — of our own sex, shall I say? — are not yet foolishly vain of their caprices; but the former class I must refer for counsel to treatises on intellectual and moral philosophy, and with the latter I have little sympathy. It may not be amiss, however, for each one of us to examine our own habits of judging and acting, with reference to this subject. There can be nothing like the perfection of mind or of heart, when prejudices, of whatever sort, are tolerated; and to become the slave of caprice, is a thing so utterly contemptible, that every individual, of sound mind, must view it with sufficient disgust.

PRINCIPLE, as opposed to *policy* and *artifice*, has respect to the honorable and the fair. I know not whether the term policy may be regarded as necessarily and uniformly opposed to open, honest dealing; but I believe there is a sense in which it is compatible with it. In this acceptation it can mean nothing else than skill to discover and to seize the fittest occasions, and dexterity in applying the means best adapted for effecting a desired purpose. It is rather opposed to heedlessness and stupidity, than to the honorable and just. Used in this sense, I am certainly no enemy to policy. There are certain opportunities for advancing our interests, which providence puts in our way, and which we are at liberty to seize and profit by, or to neglect and lose. Here lies the fair province of success in trade, in civil government and economy, in the department of social intercourse and of domestic training. It is a sort of happy tact, which is the principal instrument and the best guarantee of success. But the line of demarcation between tact and trick is often so narrow as not to be discovered; or, if discovered, not to prove an effectual barrier. Hence the peculiar temptations attending such professions as require uncommon shrewdness. How can one be an honest lawyer, an honest merchant, or an honest woman of fashion? How be polite, how humane even, and adhere strictly to truth? I ask these questions, not to appal, but simply to point out the quicksands to which the enterprising and gifted are peculiarly exposed.

On this subject there can be but one rule. *The true and the honorable must be kept to*, consequences to the contrary notwithstanding. If we have not skill enough to practise honest policy, without passing the fearful limit, and finding ourselves on the enchanted ground of duplicity and falsehood, we must be content to be plain and simple in our character and conduct. I would far sooner wear the drab than the rouge. I would far sooner be the honest, or, if you please, the stupid German, than the witty and accomplished, if I must be the false Françoise.

Lastly, we are to consider PRINCIPLE as opposed to *dishonesty* and *impiety*. I know not in what language adequately to set forth the importance of this branch of our subject. It is that on which I am desirous the chief stress of this effort should rest. Engaged as I have long been in devising schemes for the improvement of mind and morals, especially among my own sex, and in testing these schemes by actual experiment, I am brought at length to feel that the axe is not yet effectually laid at the root of the tree. It has ever been our theory, a theory which we have endeavored to reduce to practice, that the end of education could in no satisfactory manner be secured, except in proportion to the advancement of moral culture. As a community, we have been felicitating ourselves for the last twenty years, upon the diffusion and happy influence of Sabbath schools and bible classes, as efficient and almost omnipotent agencies in securing the advancement of morals. We do not say that these means have not been fraught with immense good. But we find yet, on every hand, the sad impress of moral ruin. We find corruption under the fairest exterior — the venom of the serpent under the guise of dove-like innocence. We find that weakness and instability in the professed, and, in the judgment of charity, the real Christian, which often betrays into dissembling, equivocation, and wrong. Whence arises this laxity of morals, this weakness of virtue, that the disciples of Jesus should thus succumb under temptations so inconsiderable in comparison with those their Master withstood? It was not so in the times of the apostles; it was not so in the times of the pilgrim fathers; it was not so, unless we are under the influence of a prejudice, in the times of our grandfathers. It is true, professors of religion were then more rare, and it is to be expected, perhaps it may be said, that they would be of more sterling piety. But are not the principles of the gospel the same in every age, and in every heart? Can they admit, under any circumstances, of any compromise with fraud and deceit? We cannot feel that it is so. The duty we owe our fellow-men, to love them *as ourselves* — to God, to give him the supreme affection of our hearts, and to express this affection by scrupulously keeping his commandments, must be *everywhere and at all times* the same.

Allow me, then, in conclusion, my dear young friends, to intreat your attention to this subject. Do not break God's law by violating the rights of your fellow-beings, in however small a degree, or indirect a form. Do not insult the majesty of Heaven, by thinking to beguile him of what is due more immediately to himself. Examine the precepts, one by one, as contained in that admirable code, the moral law, and exhibited, and clearly illustrated, in the spirituality of their application, in the New Testament.

If there were but one thing I were permitted to enjoin upon you, as the last legacy of an affectionate instructress, it should be this: Give yourselves up entirely and implicitly to the influence of strict *religious principle.* In your intercourse with each other, in the distribution of your time, in the appropriation of your money, in the employment of your genius, in the occupations of the Sabbath, in the direction of the thoughts, in the bestowment of the affections, let everything be done upon *christian principle*. Let the law of Christ be absolute and ultimate, over all your resources, and in all the details of life. · So may you hope to escape the pollutions of the world, and to awake at length in the glorious likeness of the Redeemer, to share the blessing himself pronounced upon the pure in heart.

THE END.

Titles in this Series

Edited with an Introduction by Carolyn De Swarte Gifford

  a. Buckley, James Monroe. "Because They Are Women, and Other Editorials From the Christian Advocate on the Admission of Women to the General Conference." New York: 1891.

  b. Hughey, George W. *The Admission of Women to the General Conference: A Reply to Dr. Buckley's Pamphlet "Because They Are women."* Chicago: 1891

  c. Kynett, Alpha J. "Our Laity and Their Equal Rights Without Distinction of Sex in the Methodist Episcopal Church." Cincinnati: 1896

  d. Palmer, Willis. "Are Women Eligible as Lay Delegates to the General Conference?" New Richmond, Ohio: 1888.

4. *The Defense of Women's Rights to Ordination in the Methodist Episcopal Church*
Edited with an Introduction by Carolyn De Swarte Gifford

  a. Willard, Francis E. *Woman in the Pulpit.* Chicago: 1889.

  b. Warren, William Fairfield. "The Dual Human Unit: The Relations of Men and Women According to the Sociological Teachings of Holy Scripture" in *Constitutional Law Questions Now Pending in the*

Methodist Episcopal Church. Cincinnati: 1894.

5. *The Ideal of "The New Woman" According to the Woman's Christian Temperance Union*
Edited with an Introduction by Carolyn De Swarte Gifford

    a. Willard, Francis E. *How to Win: A Book for Girls*. New York: 1886.

    b. Willard, Francis E. *Do Everything: A Handbook for the World's White Ribboners*. Chicago: c. 1895.

    c. Willard, Francis E. *Home Protection Manual: Containing an Argument for the Temperance Ballot for Women and How to Obtain It as a Means of Home Protection*. New York: 1879.

6. *The Nineteenth-Century American Preacher's Wife*
Edited with an Introduction by Carolyn De Swarte Gifford

    a. Eaton, Herrick M. *The Itinerant's Wife: Her Qualifications, Duties, Trials, and Rewards*. New York: 1851

    b. Tucker, Mary Orne. *Itinerant Preaching in the Early Days of Methodism*. Boston: 1872.

7. John Holmes Acornley. *The Colored Lady Evangelist, Being the Life, Labors and Experiences of Mrs. Harriet A. Baker*. Brooklyn: 1892

8. C. W. Andrews. *Memoir of Mrs. Ann R. Page.* New York: 1856.

9. Francis J. Baker. *The Story of the Woman's Foreign Missionary Society of the Methodist Episcopal Church, 1869–1895.* Cincinnati: 1896.

10. Joanna Bethune. *The Power of Faith, Exemplified in the Life and Writings of the Late Mrs. Isabella Graham.* New York: 1843.

11. George Brown. *The Lady Preacher: Or, the Life and Labors of Mrs. Hannah Reeves, Late the Wife of the Rev. William Reeves of the Methodist Church.* Springfield, Ohio: 1870.

12. Oswald E. Brown and Anna M. Brown. *Life and Letters of Laura Askew Haygood.* Nashville: 1904.

13. Fanny Jackson–Coppin. *Reminiscences of School Life, and Hints on Teaching.* Philadelphia: 1913.

14. John O. Foster. *Life and Labors of Mrs. Maggie Newton Van Cott, the First Lady Licensed to Preach in the Methodist Episcopal Church in the United States.* Cincinnati: 1872.

15. Marietta Holley. *Samantha Among the Brethren, By Josiah Allen's Wife.* New York: 1890.

16. Isabelle Horton. *High Adventure: Life of Lucy Rider Meyer.* New York: 1928.

17. Sarah R. Ingraham. *Walks of Usefulness. Or, Reminiscences of Mrs. Margaret Prior*. New York: 1843.

18. James D. Knowles. *Memoir of Mrs. Ann H. Judson, Late Missionary to Burmah. Including a History of the American Baptist Mission in the Burman Empire*. Boston: 1831.

19. Mrs. Robert W. MacDonell. *Belle Harris Bennett, Her Life Work*. Nashville: 1928.

20. Helen Barrett Montgomery. *Western Women in Eastern Lands. An Outline Study of Fifty Years of Woman's Work in Foreign Missions*. New York: 1910.

21. Elizabeth Mason North. *Consecrated Talents: Or, the Life of Mrs. Mary W. Mason*. New York: 1870.

22. George L. Prentiss. *The Life and Letters of Elizabeth Prentiss*. New York: 1882.

23. Lydia Sexton. *Autobiography of Lydia Sexton. The Story of Her Life Through a Period of Over Seventy-Two Years from 1799–1872. Her Early Privations, Adventures, and Reminiscences*. Dayton, Ohio: 1882.

24. Sarah Sleeper. *Memoir of the Late Martha Hazeltine Smith*. Boston: 1843.

25. Amanda Berry Smith. *An Autobiography. The Story of the Lord's Dealings with Mrs. Amanda Smith, the Colored Evangelist, Containing an Account of Her Life Work of Faith, and Her Travels in America, England, Ireland, Scotland, India and Africa, as an Independent Missionary.* Chicago: 1893.

26. Lee Anna Starr. *The Bible Status of Woman.* New York: 1926.

27. Abel Stevens. *The Women of Methodism: Its Three Foundresses, Susanna Wesley, The Countess of Huntingdon, and Barbara Heck; with Sketches of Their Female Associates and Successors in the Early History of the Denomination.* New York: 1869.

28. Clara A. Swain. *A Glimpse of India, Being a Collection of Extracts from the Letters of Dr. Clara A. Swain, First Medical Missionary to India of the Woman's Foreign Missionary Society of the Methodist Episcopal Church in America.* New York: 1909.

29. James Mills Thoburn. *Life of Isabella Thoburn.* New York: 1903.

30. Alexander Harrison Tuttle, ed. *Mary Porter Gamewell and Her Story of the Siege in Peking.* New York: 1907.

31. Uldine Utley. *Why I Am a Preacher. A Plain Answer to an Oft-Repeated Question*. New York: 1931.

32. Alma White. *Looking Back from Beulah*. Zarephath, New Jersey: 1902.

33. Mary Culler White. *The Portal of Wonderland; The Life–Story of Alice Culler Cobb*. New York: c. 1925.

34. Elizabeth Wilson. *Fifty Years of Association Work Among Young Women, 1866–1916*. New York: 1916.

35. Miron Winslow. *Memoir of Mrs. Harriet L. Winslow, Thirteen Years a Member of the American Mission in Ceylon*. New York: 1840.

36. Annie Turner Wittenmeyer. *Women's Work for Jesus*. New York: 1873.